super cool drinks

super cool drinks

michael van straten

MITCHELL BEAZLEY

Super Cool Drinks

by Michael van Straten

First published in Great Britain in 2004 by

Mitchell Beazley, an imprint of Octopus Publishing

Group Limited, 2–4 Heron Quays, London E14 4JP.

A CIP catalogue record for this book is available from the British Library.

ISBN: 1 84000 773 7

The author and publishers will be grateful for any information that will assist them in keeping
future editions up-to-date. Although all reasonable care has been taken in the preparation of this
book, neither the publishers, editors nor the author can accept any liability for any consequences
arising from the use thereof, or the information contained therein.

Commissioning Editor: Rebecca Spry

Executive Art Editor: Yasia Williams

Design: Plan B Design

Editor: Jamie Ambrose

Photographer: Peter Cassidy

Stylist: Louise Mackaness

Proof reader: Julie Tolley

Production: Gilbert Francourt

Index: John Noble

Typeset in Myriad MM

Printed and bound by Toppan Printing Company in China

Contents

Introduction

Water has always been an important part of natural therapies. From the most ancient times, water has been used both externally and internally as a way of promoting and maintaining good health. The healing properties of many natural springs and spas are legendary, and "taking the waters" is still part of the therapeutic approach in Europe's spas.

Health experts maintain that we should be drinking pints of water every day and avoiding excessive amounts of coffee, tea, and alcohol. There's no doubt that not drinking enough liquids can be a major health hazard – but who really wants to drink eight or ten glasses of plain water every day? Thankfully, this book offers you an amazing selection of alternatives to "Adam's Ale": cooling drinks that not only taste delicious but also have specific therapeutic benefits. Many of them are acceptable substitutes for plain water and will make reaching your daily fluid targets a more pleasant business.

In general terms, dehydration is seriously bad news. It can have an impact on how you look as well as how you feel. Whether it's the drying effect of central heating or air conditioning, or just a long spell of dry weather, your body will suffer if you don't give it enough fluid. Bearing in mind that the average office has an atmosphere drier than the Sahara Desert and that most modern homes are now hermetically sealed boxes with double glazing, thermal insulation, and draught exclusion, the risks of dehydration are dramatically greater than they were twenty or thirty years ago.

This book encourages you to drink more liquids and thus reduce the side-effects of dehydration. But it also gives recipes for drinks that are rich in nutrients and natural plant chemicals, which have specific health benefits. One of the first organs to suffer from dehydration is your skin; it soon becomes dry, flaky, irritable, itchy, and eventually begins to split and crack. It's vital that anyone with general skin problems should moisturize from the inside, with plenty of liquids, as well as on the outside. Constipation, kidney stones, urinary infections, headaches, migraine, sinus problems, itchy eyes, and a sore, fissured tongue can all be linked to not drinking enough.

In this book, you'll find drinks that stimulate the body's cleansing processes by improving the function of the kidneys, liver, and digestive system. There are cooling drinks that replace fluid lost through sweating and help lower the body's temperature. A healthy diet contains at least five portions of fruit and vegetables a day; a fresh fruit or vegetable drink counts for at least one of these, but it also provides enormous benefits, thanks to the protective plant chemicals that are only present in raw produce. Getting them from pills is not the same as consuming berries, cherries, and other dark fruits and vegetables.

Your immune system is a common casualty of twenty-first-century living. Too much stress, not enough sleep, and excessive consumption of poor nutrient-quality processed foods mean you're much more likely to catch bugs and to be an easy target for every stray virus as you will have a weakened immune system. For this reason, I have included drinks that increase resistance and boost your natural immunity. And if you're unlucky enough to get ill, have an accident, need surgery or live through an exhausting and debilitating period at work or home, your vitality will be in need of restoration. All the ingredients you need for recovery can be found in the chapter on restorative drinks.

We're living through an epidemic of obesity. In the slimming chapter, you'll find health-giving drinks that can help you shift excess weight and keep you away from dangerous extreme dietary regimes.

Yet the magic factor we all seek to improve is vitality. Overcoming chronic fatigue and lethargy is a major quest for many people, as constant tiredness ruins career prospects, personal relationships, health, and happiness. The drinks in the first chapter are the ideal aid to beating this problem.

Vita

lity
Drinks

Fatigue and exhaustion are probably among the most common reasons why people visit a doctor, and this is nearly always a fruitless exercise. Of course, you should be checked out to make sure you don't have a thyroid problem, that you're not anaemic, or that there isn't some other underlying medical cause. For the majority of people, however, it's a question of simply learning to eat better. Avoid the high-sugar, refined-carbohydrate foods that give you an instant but short-lived lift, a massive outpouring of insulin and, over time, increase your risk of diabetes, obesity, and heart disease. Instead, try these recipes for drinks that combine slow- and quick-release energy, reduce the risk of diabetes, and help boost your vitality and improve your overall health at the same time.

Lychee, Buttermilk, and Honey

If you've only ever had tinned lychees in syrup in your local Chinese restaurant, then this smoothie will be a revelation. Fresh lychees are a totally different taste sensation. They have the most delicate flavour and are also a useful source of nutrients. Using buttermilk rather than yoghurt or ordinary milk provides a different texture as well as an unusual taste to this energy-giving recipe.

Serves 1-2
10 lychees
125ml or 4fl oz buttermilk
3 level tbsp runny honey
2 redcurrant sprigs (for garnish)

1 Peel and stone the lychees. Put the flesh into a blender and whizz.
2 Add the buttermilk and honey and whizz again.
3 Serve with the redcurrant sprigs draped over the edge of the glasses.

vital statistics

Lychees are a good source of **vitamin C**, but they also contain some **calcium**, **potassium**, and **phosphorus**, all of which are important for **energy** conversion as well as **healthy** bones. The protein and **extra calcium** from the **buttermilk**, as well as its extremely low **sugar** content, means you avoid the **insulin** rush of high-sugar energy-boosters; instead, you benefit from a sustained increase in your general **vitality**.

Guava Delight

This smoothie is the ideal combination of instant and slow-release energy with the added sting in the tail of the Brazilian rain-forest herb known as guarana. Whether you're sitting in a high-powered meeting, working at your computer or going off to play a weekend game of football or tennis, this is the way to give your vitality a healthy boost. All the tropical fruits are rich in natural sugars for an instant lift, while the banana provides some protein and lots of complex carbohydrates for a more gradual release of usable energy.

Serves 1-2
1 guava
1 mango
1 banana
5g or 1 tsp guarana powder

1 Peel the guava.
2 Peel and stone the mango.
3 Put them both through a juicer.
4 Peel the banana and whizz with the juice in a blender or food processor.
5 Add the guarana and whizz again.
6 Chill before serving.

vital statistics

Guavas and mangoes are rich in betacarotene, **vitamin C**, natural sugars, and lots of protective **antioxidants**. The **banana** contains large amounts of **potassium**, which is important to prevent cramp during sustained muscular activity. So if you need your extra vitality for **sport** and **exercise**, this is the drink for you; it also helps maintain a high level of mental activity over long periods of time. Using the **guarana** adds the age-old wisdom of rain-forest Indian medicine to this modern-day vitality drink.

Honeyed Iced Tea

The complex flavours of this unusual iced tea make it the perfect refreshing and revitalizing drink on a hot summer's day. It does sound like a lot of trouble, but during a hot spell it's worth making double the quantity and putting it in a covered jug in the refrigerator, where it will easily keep for two or three days. It's not the nutrients that are important here; the essential oils in the spices are what provide a vitality boost.

Serves 4
About 600ml or 20fl oz water
5 Earl Grey tea bags
4 cinnamon sticks
4 cardamom pods
1 tsp black peppercorns
1 tbsp coriander seeds
1 tbsp runny honey

1 Boil the water.
2 Add the tea bags, leave for ten minutes, then remove.
3 Break the cinnamon sticks into roughly 2.5cm (one-inch) pieces.
4 Crush the cardamom pods, peppercorns, and coriander seeds.
5 Put the tea into a large, heatproof bowl, add the spices, and leave for at least four hours.
6 Strain into a saucepan.
7 Reheat and stir in the honey.
8 Leave to cool before serving.

vital statistics

Tea on its own is a valuable and protective **antioxidant**, and this is enhanced by the addition of the **bergamot oil** that is used to make Earl Grey. **Cinnamon, cardamom,** and **coriander** are all **energizing** immune-boosting, and **stimulating** spices, and peppercorns help to stimulate the **circulation**. Just what you need to **boost** your flagging **spirits** on a hot, humid, and tiring afternoon.

Wake-up Call

Here's a combination of quick- and slow-release energy, essential nutrients, protein, and fibre that is a great early-morning starter or a before-sport booster for your vitality. Most women I know think peanut butter is one of the greatest sins, as it must be fattening. This is far from the truth. Peanut butter helps in any weight-loss plan as it provides slow-release energies which prevent a fall in blood sugar and a craving for sweet things. Furthermore, because peanuts are broken down very slowly into energy-giving sugars, the nuts and peanut butter help protect against adult-onset diabetes.

Serves 1-2
2 eating apples
1 pear
2 bananas
1 heaped tbsp smooth peanut butter
150ml or 5fl oz crème fraîche
1 tsp cinnamon

1 Wash, core, and quarter the apples and pear.
2 Peel the bananas.
3 Put the apples and pear through a juicer.
4 Put the juice, peanut butter, crème fraîche, and banana into a liquidizer and whizz.
5 Serve with the cinnamon sprinkled on top.

vital statistics

It's the **protein** and plant **lignins** in the **peanuts** that provide slow-release energy and help **reduce cholesterol** and **insulin** levels. Add the banana for more slow-release energy and lots of potassium to prevent cramp during **exercise**, and you've got the basis of this great **vitality** drink. The rest of the **fruit** provides **vitamin C** and soluble fibre, while the **crème fraîche** gives you even more **calcium** and B **vitamins**. A delicious feast of nutrients.

Spiced Smoothie

One of the most common causes of chronic fatigue is a deficiency of zinc and since this is a mineral often in short supply in the convenience-food diet so many of us live on today, the extra zinc supplied by pumpkin seeds is often the first step on the road to feeling more vital and healthy. Often lack of vitality is caused by poor resistance and repeated infections such as flu, sore throats, coughs, and colds. Regular consumption of live yoghurt is a tremendous boost to the immune system, thanks to the beneficial bacteria it contains.

Serves 1-2
300ml or 10fl oz plain live yoghurt
1 tbsp tahini
Half a tsp allspice
A little milk (optional), for thinning
Ice-cubes
1 tsp pumpkin seeds

1 Put the yoghurt, tahini, and allspice in a blender or food processor and whizz until combined.
2 Thin with the milk until you achieve the consistency you require.
3 Serve over ice-cubes with the pumpkin seeds scattered on top.

vital statistics

Live **yoghurt** is not only an excellent source of **calcium** for strong and healthy bones, but it is the best source of the **probiotic bacteria** responsible for producing essential **B vitamins** that nourish the nervous system and **help** banish anxiety, **stress**, and **fatigue**. Add the slow-release **calories** and even more calcium from the **tahini**, the **zinc** from the **pumpkin seeds**, and the mood-enhancing benefits of allspice, and you've got a great recipe for improved vitality.

Pawpaw and Ginger Refresher

If you want to ginger up your vitality, then this is the drink for you. The ginger accentuates the delicious flavour of the pawpaw but also adds its own distinctive boost to this drink. This is a wonderful recipe for a lazy Sunday morning when you read the papers, and just the thing to have before your weekly treat of a real English breakfast. The digestive enzyme papaine in the pawpaws is a great aid to the digestion of high-protein foods.

Serves 1-2
3 pawpaws
Half a tsp ground ginger
Water (for diluting)

1   Peel and deseed the pawpaws.
2   Put into a blender or food processor with the ground ginger and whizz until smooth.
3   Dilute with water to your desired consistency.
4   Chill well before serving.

vital statistics

As well as being rich in **vitamin C**, **pawpaws** provide plenty of **betacarotene**, lots of **flavonoids**, and a surprisingly high amount of the essential mineral **magnesium**. The natural **gingerols** and **zingiberenes** in ginger **boost** the circulatory system and give an almost instant **lift** to your vitality. As an additional benefit, this is ideal for any pregnant woman suffering from early morning sickness.

Ginger It Up

This spicy variation on the traditional Indian lassi will give an instant lift to anybody's flagging vitality. The stimulating effects of ginger, the beneficial bacteria in the yoghurt and the digestive benefits of mint all work together to give your vitality a welcome lift just when you need one.

Serves 1-2
4cm or 1$\frac{1}{2}$-inch piece fresh ginger
250ml or 9fl oz plain live yoghurt
About 10 mint leaves
   (and 4 small sprigs for garnish)
Chilled sparkling mineral water,
   to taste

1 Peel and grate the ginger.
2 Put the yoghurt, ginger, and mint leaves in a blender and whizz until smooth.
3 Mix with the mineral water to your desired consistency.
4 Pour into glasses and serve with the mint sprigs floating on top.

vital statistics

It's the circulatory **enhancing** effect of **zingiberene** and the gingerols that make **ginger** such a powerful stimulant. The hotness of this **spice** is offset by the coolness of the **yoghurt**, which supplies valuable quantities of **calcium**, some **protein**, **B vitamins**, and the important probiotic bacteria that are so essential for **immunity** and good **digestion**. Add the **mint**, which is the best of all natural digestive aids, and you have a **cooling** and **revitalizing** smoothie.

Apple and Beetroot Smoothie

Throughout eastern Europe, beetroot has long been regarded as a traditional vitality-boosting vegetable in folklore and conventional medicine alike. Historically, its colour associated it with being good for the blood – an observation that has been proved accurate by modern science. Combined with the live bacteria in the yoghurt, which gives a powerful boost to the natural immune system, this smoothie is the ultimate vitality drink.

Serves 1-2
3 apples
2 medium cooked beetroot
125ml or 4fl oz plain live yoghurt

1 Core the apples and quarter them and the beetroot.
2 Put through a juicer.
3 Stir in the yoghurt and serve.

vital statistics

Large amounts of folic acid reduce the levels of **homocysteine** in the circulating blood, and this action helps greatly to **protect** against heart disease. **Iron**, potassium, calcium, betacarotene, and some **vitamins** are also provided by the **beetroot**, all of which help **boost** vitality levels. The **apple juice** contains **vitamin C** and ellagic acid, both immune-boosters, and the yoghurt provides a quarter of a day's **calcium** requirements as well as the live bacteria that are so important for **effective** digestion, the synthesis of **B vitamins**, and a strong immune system.

Rum Deal

I first drank pawpaw juice served with limes and the local sugar-cane rum on a small boat in the Amazon rain forest of Brazil. Unfortunately, it tastes like the most delicious chilled fruit juice, and for somebody like me who seldom drinks alcohol, three glasses of this delicious and refreshing drink left me stupefied – not revitalized. However, I've learned from my mistake that using lots of ice and making one drink last a long time on a very hot day is both cooling and revitalizing. It's also very sociable, so try it at your next barbecue.

Serves 1-2
3 pawpaws
2 limes
4 tbsp white rum
Crushed ice

1. Peel the pawpaws, scrape out the seeds, and then juice them.
2. Squeeze the juice from the limes. Add to the pawpaw juice, along with the rum.
3. Serve over crushed ice.

vital statistics

In fact, this drink is perfect before a **barbecue**, which tends to be a bit heavy on meat, as the digestive **enzyme** papaine helps the breakdown and absorption of meat proteins. Add lots of **vitamin C** from the lime as well as all the **immune-boosting** nutrients in the **pawpaws** and you've got a real boost to your **vitality** – as long as you don't overdo the rum…

A Punch of Power

Here's another super vitality juice with plenty of essential nutrients and some surprisingly potent natural phytochemicals from the coriander and spinach. It makes an excellent drink for physically active people as it provides a boost of instant energy from the natural sugars in the carrots and kiwi fruit. It is also a good source of potassium – so important for muscle performance.

Serves 1-2

4 carrots
1 kiwi fruit, washed
1 small handful fresh coriander, with stems
1 handful baby spinach leaves

1 Wash all the ingredients and peel, top, and tail the carrots (unless they're organic). Leave the kiwi fruit unpeeled.
2 Put all the ingredients into a juicer, reserving a few coriander leaves.
3 Mix well and serve with coriander leaves on top.

vital statistics

This vitality drinks provides a double dose of **betacarotene** and **potassium** from the **carrots** and **kiwi fruit**, along with extra magnesium and plenty of **vitamin C**. The **spinach** adds extra **carotenoids** and a powerful **boost** of cancer-fighting plant chemicals. The **coriander** contains heart- and circulatory-**protective** coumarins and also an effective **antiseptic** essential oil called linalol.

ling
Drinks

You may think that air-conditioning is the ultimate luxury, keeping people cool on hot, uncomfortable days. Unfortunately keeping cool in this way has its price – the typical office building now has an atmosphere that is drier than the Sahara Desert! This wreaks havoc with skin and hair, and can have serious consequences for anyone with breathing problems. The consequent dehydration, aggravated by lack of fluid intake, also increases the risk of kidney stones, urinary infections, and chronic constipation. So turn off the air-conditioning, open the windows, get an old-fashioned fan, and use these delightful cooling drinks to keep you well-hydrated and supremely comfortable.

Pink Grapefruit Punch

This is a great pre-barbecue ice-breaker to be sipped gently under the shade of a large garden umbrella – even if it is to keep off the rain! But who needs an excuse to enjoy any form of Pimm's? It's cool, refreshing, and, in moderation, extremely good for your health. You'll love the interesting mixture of Pimm's and the sweet tartness of good pink grapefruit. This punch will certainly cool you down on a hot day – and even when it's grey, wet, and miserable, it'll cheer you up with its wonderful suggestions of smooth, green lawns and summer sunshine.

For 6 party-loving people
4 pink grapefruit
Ice-cubes
Half a bottle of Pimm's
Half a bottle of good sparkling wine
Soda water
1 lemon

1 Squeeze the juice from the grapefruit using a citrus-citrus fruit or hand-held juicer (DON'T put them through a juicing machine made for harder fruits).
2 Put some ice into a large punch-bowl.
3 Over the ice, pour the juice, Pimm's, and sparkling wine.
4 Stir well, then top up with soda water.
5 Slice the lemon thinly and use it as a garnish.

vital statistics
Pink grapefruit provides abundant amounts of **vitamin C** and also some **betacarotene**. Grapefruit contains **bioflavonoids**, too, which play an important part in protecting the inside walls of **veins** and **arteries**. Though red wine is reputedly the heart-protector, all **alcoholic drinks** are **good** for your **heart and circulation** as long as you don't consume them to excess. Some prescribed medicines react badly with grapefruit and **grapefruit** juice, so check the leaflets of any **medicines** you've been given by your doctor; if you're not sure, ask your pharmacist.

Blackberry Bellini

What could be more cooling than this deliciously healthy and refreshing drink? Most people enjoy a glass of Bucks Fizz, but this "Hedgerow Fizz" is quite different. If picking your own blackberries, make sure they're really ripe; otherwise they can be sour and bitter. If they're wild, avoid those growing by the roadside as they will be contaminated with exhaust fumes. The sharp, clean taste of mint is especially refreshing – even more so combined with the heady bubbles of Champagne or sparkling wine.

Serves 1-2

225g or 8oz fresh or frozen blackberries

Half a bottle of chilled, medium-sweet Champagne or sparkling wine

Two sprigs of mint

1 Defrost the fruit, if necessary. Wash it if fresh.
2 Put into a blender and whizz until smooth.
3 Push through a sieve to remove the pips.
4 Pour the Champagne or wine into chilled glasses.
5 Top with the blackberry juice and garnish with the mint.

vital statistics

Not only are **blackberries** an excellent source of **vitamin C**, they also provide substantial amounts of **vitamin E**, so this drink has health benefits as well. Like all the very dark-coloured fruits, blackberries are a **rich source** of **protective antioxidants**, and these properties are further enhanced by the cardioprotective **benefits** of the alcohol.

Coriander Special

It's not always easy to find uncooked beetroot, but it's certainly worth the effort as the combination of apple and beetroot juice is as tasty as it is unusual. The distinctive flavour of celery blends well with the other ingredients, and the tartness of lime and cranberry offsets the sweetness of the beetroot. This is a perfect drink for all seasons.

Serves 1-2
1 lime
1 stalk celery
Half a handful coriander leaves
1 small uncooked beetroot,
   preferably with leaves
75ml or about 3fl oz apple juice
75ml or about 3fl oz cranberry juice

1 Squeeze the juice from the lime and reserve.
2 Put the celery, coriander, and beetroot through a juicer.
3 Mix in the lime, apple, and cranberry juice to serve.

vital statistics

This juice has an extremely high **vitamin C** content, thanks to the lime, cranberry, and apple, so it also acts as an **immune-booster**. Beetroot has long been a traditional favourite remedy for all kinds of **blood disorders**, particularly anaemia, which causes chronic **fatigue**. They're a major source of betacarotene, **vitamins B$_6$** and **C**, folic acid, iron, and potassium, and they work well as a **blood-booster**. The addition of **cranberry** juice adds urinary protection, making this drink ideal for anyone with **recurrent** cystitis.

Mint Cooler

To be honest, this is just a fancy name for mint tea, but for a unique taste you should use the real peppermint, *Mentha piperita*. Mints are so easy to grow, even in pots on your doorstep or window-sill, that it's worth having your own selection for a wide variety of flavours. Moroccan mint, spearmint, lemon mint or (for something really unusual) ginger mint, are all good as teas or used to flavour other foods. Mint is a traditional ingredient of many summer cooling drinks, particularly the juleps of the southern United States – perfect on a warm summer's evening sitting on the veranda in your rocking chair.

Serves 4
3 large sprigs of peppermint
600ml or 20fl oz boiling water
1 level tbsp brown caster sugar

1 Finely chop the peppermint leaves and stalks, leaving two small sprigs aside.
2 Use the water to make tea with the leaves in the normal way.
3 Add the sugar to the teapot.
4 Leave to cool completely.
5 Strain and transfer to a glass jug.
6 Chill before serving, garnished with the reserved mint sprigs.

vital statistics

All the **mints** have **medicinal** properties, related mostly to their content of **menthol**. The Japanese have cultivated mint for 4,000 years just to extract the menthol, and in Egypt, remnants of mint have been found in **pharaohs' tombs** that are 3,000 years old. You'll find references to mint in **Greek mythology** and in the Bible. **Essential oils** from mint are still used medicinally as one of the **most effective** treatments for indigestion.

Cucumber and Strawberry Frappé

Strawberries and sunshine go together like bread and jam. When mixed with ice-cold yoghurt and cooling cucumber, they help create this wonderful summer drink. Freshly ground black pepper helps bring out the succulent flavour of strawberries – don't knock it until you've tried it.

Serves 1-2
1 large cucumber
6 large strawberries
About 300ml or 10fl oz plain live yoghurt
Freshly ground black pepper

1 Peel, deseed, and cube the cucumber.
2 Wash and hull the strawberries.
3 Put both fruits into a blender or food processor with the yoghurt.
4 Whizz until smooth.
5 Add the pepper to taste and serve.

vital statistics
Betacarotene, vitamin C, and specific **phytochemicals** in the **strawberries** give this drink valuable **anti-arthritic** properties, while the high calcium content of the yoghurt helps all bone and **joint conditions**. It's important to use live **yoghurt**, as this is the only type that contains active **probiotic bacteria**. These friendly bugs help to improve digestion, synthesize some of the B vitamins, and **boost** your natural immunity.

Mango Lassi

As the lassi originates from India, it's hardly surprising that this is a supercool drink. Though you can make it with normal dairy yoghurt, soya yoghurt is used here to provide hormone regulation and to help build strong bones. Just thinking about the smell and flavour of mangoes is enough to conjure up tropical images, but eating them is even better, as they not only taste sublime but provide lots of essential nutrients. Drink this chilled if you must, but if it's too cold, you lose both aroma and flavour.

Serves 1-2
2 mangoes
225ml or 8fl oz soya yoghurt

1 Peel, stone, and cube the mango flesh.
2 Put into a blender with the yoghurt and whizz until smooth.
3 Chill, if necessary, before serving.

vital statistics

Mangoes are a rich source of **health-protective betacarotenes** and other age-defying **carotenoids** and **flavonoids**. They're also rich in **potassium** for heart protection and in **vitamin C** for your immune defences. The **phytoestrogens** in soya are known to be part of the reason why Asian women have less **breast cancer**, less osteoporosis, and hardly ever suffer the discomfort of menopausal **hot flushes**.

Strawberry Sundae

This is a wonderful milk shake and, without the vodka, extremely healthy for children. It provides lots of nutrients and is a great way of getting good food and vital calories into anyone unable to eat due to mouth or throat problems, or recovering from surgery or major illness. It's important to blend the ingredients together long enough to remove all lumps so that it can be drunk through a straw. It's also best to use ingredients straight from the fridge rather than chilling the shake afterwards, as the milk and crème fraîche may separate a bit.

Serves 1-2
400g or 14oz strawberries
Half a standard wine glass of vodka (optional)
125ml or 4fl oz crème fraîche
75ml or about 3fl oz full-fat milk

1 Keeping two of the strawberries aside, hull the rest and put them into a blender with the vodka, crème fraîche, and milk. Whizz until smooth, thinning with more milk if necessary.
2 Serve with the reserved strawberries, almost halved and sitting over the rim of the glasses.

vital statistics

The combination of **crème fraîche** and milk provides lots of **calcium**, protein, potassium, **B vitamins**, and some **vitamin A**, and the **strawberries** add plenty of **vitamin C**, some fibre, and folic acid, making this an excellent **nutritional** package. This drink is a good immune-booster and particularly important for all **children** and **women** as it helps protect and build **strong bones**. During the winter months, you can substitute frozen **strawberries**, but make sure they defrost first. Even though they lose some of their vitamin C, they're still extremely **healthy**.

Rosewater with Melon

Although you can buy rosewater from good cookery shops, delis, and pharmacies, it's not widely used. It's even more unusual for people to eat rose petals. But these wonderful plants have been used medicinally for more than 5,000 years by the Chinese as well as in the ancient cultures of Greece and Rome. Rose-petal jam has been enjoyed as a gourmet treat since the days of Elizabeth I – now here's *your* chance to see what all the fuss is about. Remember: only roses that smell good will taste good; also pick the petals before they start to fall by themselves. Like all melon drinks, this is a delicious cooler, enhanced by the heady aroma and taste of roses.

Serves 2
1 small melon (any type will do)
200ml or 7fl oz rosewater
Small handful rose petals

1 Peel and deseed the melon.
2 Cut into chunks and whizz in a blender or food processor.
3 Add the rosewater and whizz again briefly.
4 Wash the rose petals and put half in the bottom of two glasses.
5 Top with the juice.
6 Serve with the rest of the petals scattered on top.

vital statistics

Rose petals contain **astringent** cleansing and **antiseptic** tannins as well as the volatile **essential oils** which provide the **perfume**. Most **melons** are not rich in nutrients, although the **deep-yellow** and orange varieties contain **betacarotene** and other **carotenoids**. Though you can use any melon for this recipe, the strongly **aromatic varieties** do tend to submerge the more **delicate** perfume and **flavour** of the **rosewater** and petals.

Sundae Tea

Mint and ice-cream may not sound like the perfect bedfellows, but in fact the flavours go brilliantly together, because ice-cream is such a versatile medium. You can even combine it with garlic (which I've tried and found surprisingly good). Of course, how good this sundae is depends entirely on the quality of the ice-cream; you'll be very disappointed if you try it with cheap, non-dairy varieties. This is another treat that is great for the kids and so much healthier than a cola float. Youngsters may prefer it sweetened with maple syrup, which is a good alternative to honey. As a variation, try it with chocolate ice-cream – it's better than after-dinner mints!

Serves 2
2 peppermint tea bags
1 lemon
2 tsps runny honey
2 small scoops organic vanilla ice-cream

1 Put the tea bags into two large, heatproof glasses, cover with boiling water and leave to brew. Remove the tea bags.
2 Squeeze the juice from the lemon, add half to each glass and grate enough rind for about two tablespoons.
3 Divide the honey between the glasses and stir to dissolve.
4 Cool, then leave in the fridge to chill.
5 When ready to serve, add the ice-cream and scatter with the grated lemon rind.

vital statistics

Real dairy ice-cream is a **healthy** occasional treat, as it provides plenty of **calcium** and **potassium**. Non-dairy ice-cream may be made with animal fats and **hydrogenated** vegetable fats, which are both extremely unhealthy. **Dairy ice-cream** does contain around 4g saturated fat per 100g, and while this is little compared with sausages, meat pies, and other manufactured meat products, it's still enough to suggest that you **avoid overindulgence**. The **natural oils** from the **peppermint** tea do improve digestion, so this is a good alternative to a dessert.

Mmmmm...

What could be more refreshing than this combination of melon and mangoes, two of the most succulent of summer fruits? Separately, both enjoy folklore reputations for being soothing and cooling, but when they're combined with the extra flavour of mint, they make a wonderful summer cooler. The mango is a favourite in Indian Ayurvedic medicine, where it's widely prescribed as a cooling food for the relief of fevers.

Serves 2-3
2 mangoes
1 cantaloupe melon
2 sprigs of mint

1 Peel the mangoes and remove the stones.
2 Peel and deseed the melon.
3 Put the fruits through a juicer (or into a blender) and whizz until very smooth, adding a little water if the fruit isn't breaking down.
4 Serve garnished with the mint.

Note
If you're using a blender rather than a juicer, the fruit will need to be *very* ripe.

vital statistics

Nutritionally, the high **betacarotene** content of **both fruits** serves a dual purpose. Some is converted by the body into **vitamin A** while the rest is utilized as betacarotene for individual cell **protection**. All the **carotenoids** are exceptionally valuable as part of the **body's defence** mechanisms against ageing, heart disease, and many forms of cancer. Do make sure you use this **refreshing** drink whenever the **fruits** are available as it's a real **health boost** for the whole family. This is a really **valuable** drink for children and should be used as often as possible.

Tinto de Verano

You can just imagine holding this drink in a frosted glass, sitting on your balcony looking over the blue Mediterranean from your Spanish holiday villa. It's refreshing, cooling, light, and very enjoyable. The contrasting tastes of Rioja and red vermouth, along with the delicate sweetness of lemonade (preferably homemade), make this the perfect start to your evening or enjoy it at the end of the day.

Serves 1-2

Ice-cubes
Rioja (or other Spanish red wine)
Red vermouth
Lemonade
Lemon slices

1 Put a handful of ice-cubes into a tall, thin glass.
2 Cover with red wine.
3 Add a dash of red vermouth.
4 Top up with lemonade.
5 Garnish with lemon slices.

vital statistics

You'll have noticed that there are no measurements in this recipe, and there's not much to say about its **nutritional value**, but some things are just there to be enjoyed and this is one of them. You can salve your conscience by thinking about all the **heart benefits** of drinking a couple of glasses of **red wine** a day, so four glasses of this will do you much more good than harm – as long as you **don't** use too much ice or **drive**.

Watermelon Smoothie

Watermelon is the ultimate in cooling fruits; just the sight of them piled by the roadside is enough to make you salivate. Blended here with live yoghurt, it makes the perfect cooler, whether you're at home or somewhere hot where the watermelons grow. Leave the chunks of watermelon in the fridge for at least half an hour before blending to make sure you get a cold smoothie.

Serves 2-3
1 medium watermelon
125ml or 4fl oz plain live yoghurt

1 Peel the watermelon and remove the seeds.
2 Cut into chunks.
3 Whizz in a blender or food processor with the yoghurt.

vital statistics

There are not a lot of basic **nutrients** in **watermelon**, but like all red fruits, it does contain **protective antioxidants** and small quantities of valuable **phytochemicals**. The yoghurt will provide **calcium**, and it also contains live bacteria that are beneficial to the **digestion**. One of live bacteria's major roles is **to protect** against harmful gut bacteria which cause food poisoning. If you're on holiday where it's hot enough to grow the **watermelon**, the risk of food poisoning will be there, too, so this smoothie gives you the **double benefit** of being cooling and protective.

tful
Drinks

Throughout the world there are whole populations that have less heart disease, fewer strokes, a much lower incidence of many forms of cancer, and longer life expectancy than the population of the United Kingdom. Why? The answer is unbelievably simple. All these healthy populations eat far more protective and highly nutritious fresh fruits than we do. That is why the drinks in this section have been designed to provide the maximum level of protection against the damaging free-radical chemicals that can attack every cell of the body. The natural plant chemicals that colour all berries, cherries, and darkly pigmented fresh produce are among the most powerful protective substances in nature, so drink one of these each day for the best health insurance money can buy.

Blueberry and Raspberry Crush

One serving of this will give you more protection from the ravages of free radicals than most people get in three days from the average American, northern European or UK diet. It's the free radicals that attack the body's individual cells, and it's this dangerous chemical activity that's frequently the trigger for heart disease, joint problems, diminishing eyesight, and cancer. Although you will certainly lose some of the vitamin C content from both fruits if they're frozen, the protective antioxidants aren't damaged, so you can enjoy this crush all year round.

Serves 1-2
200g or 7oz blueberries
200g or 7oz raspberries
Crushed ice

1 Wash and hull the fruit.
2 Put them both into a blender and whizz until smooth.
3 Serve in long glasses over the crushed ice.

Note
A dash of an innocuous spirit, such as vodka, could make this into a more adult drink.

vital statistics

Another **vitamin C-rich** recipe, but much more important for its exceptionally high **ORAC** score. ORAC stands for Oxygen Radical Absorption Capacity: a measure of food's ability to **neutralize** free radicals and **protect** the body from **ageing**, heart disease, **cancer**, and other **degenerative conditions**. The optimum ORAC score for a day is 5,000, but the average in the UK is barely 1,500. A large glass of this provides almost 6,000 ORACs.

Blueberry Hill

This is another extremely high-ORAC protective drink which, thanks to the cranberries, is also great for anyone with cystitis. For those with recurrent urinary infections, it is preventative as well as therapeutic. Like all the dark-coloured berries, the natural pigments provided in every glass will supply valuable amounts of essential nutrients and protective phytochemicals.

Serves 1-2

115g or 4oz frozen cranberries
115g or 4oz fresh or
  frozen raspberries
100g or 3½oz fresh blueberries
200ml or 7fl oz chilled sparkling
  mineral water

1 Defrost the frozen fruit.
2 Put all the ingredients through a juicer, or whizz in a blender or food processor until smooth.
3 Add the mineral water to taste.

vital statistics

Cranberries contain a **natural** form of vegetable mucilage which lines the walls of the urinary tract and bladder and **prevents** bacteria from growing on the surface of these tissues. As well as large quantities of **vitamin C** and **antioxidant** plant chemicals, you'll also get **potassium** for the heart, and **carotenoids** for healthy skin and eyes, together with a powerful **boost** to your **immune system**.

Passion-fruit Cup

This is a healthy, refreshing, and delicious summer drink, to be enjoyed at any time. You may be tempted to ignore this recipe, thinking that all the scooping and sieving is more trouble than it's worth, but I promise you it isn't. It has such a wonderful taste that, once you've tried it, you'll be buying passion fruit whenever you can get them. As well as their many other health-giving properties, passion fruit are an extremely mild and gentle laxative.

Serves 1-2
6 passion fruits
5ml or 1 tsp brown caster sugar
300ml or 10fl oz sparkling
  grape juice

1 Scoop the pulp out of the passion fruits and push through a sieve to remove the pips.
2 Stir in the caster sugar and mix until dissolved.
3 Add the grape juice.
4 Leave in the fridge to chill before serving.

vital statistics

As well as **betacarotene** and **vitamin C**, **passion fruit** contains many natural phytochemicals that are **antiseptic** as well as having an anti-anxiety effect. **Grape juice** possesses antioxidant properties of its own, so this combination is extremely **protective** and helps prevent premature **ageing**, **heart** and **circulatory** disease, and some forms of cancer.

What a Peach!

This really is a peach of a drink and will help keep your skin as smooth as the proverbial baby's bottom, as it's rich in youth-preserving antioxidants. It also helps boost your immune system, and as a bonus will make sure you don't get constipated. The hormone-like substances in soya yoghurt will help even out the ups and downs of hormones. Even if you're not that keen on soya products, you could add much more of the yoghurt to this drink, as the flavour will be disguised by the fruits.

Serves 1-2
4 ready-to-eat dried apricots
1 large, ripe peach
2 large oranges
30ml or 1fl oz soya yoghurt

1 Soak the apricots (even if they're 'ready to eat') for thirty minutes in just enough freshly boiled water to cover them.
2 Halve the peach, remove the stone, and put the flesh into a blender.
3 Squeeze the juice from the oranges and add to the peach flesh.
4 Drain the apricots, add to the blender, and whizz until smooth.
5 Add the yoghurt and whizz again briefly.

vital statistics
Dried apricots are an exceptional source of **betacarotene**, some of which the body uses as a **natural protective** antioxidant, some of which is converted into **vitamin A**. They are also extremely rich in **fibre** and an excellent source of **iron**. The **peach** also contributes betacarotene, while the **oranges** supply twice the daily requirement of **vitamin C**. Isoflavones (hormone-like substances) are found in all **soya** products and are helpful for **PMS**, hot flushes during the menopause, and for **protection** against osteoporosis.

Cherry Ripe

Delicious cherries: this time in an energy- and health-giving smoothie. This is the perfect breakfast for the physically active, a great brain booster if you're off to school or college, and a good source of both instant and slower-release energy. Not bad, either, to set you up for a night on the town. On a more serious note, use this recipe if you have a sore throat, cough or cold or after any form of physical injury.

Serves 1-2

200g or 7oz fresh cherries
Half a small pineapple
1 banana
1 tbsp wheatgerm
1 tbsp ground almonds
150ml or 5fl oz plain live yoghurt

1 Wash and stone the cherries.
2 Peel, core, and chop the pineapple.
3 Peel the banana.
4 Put all the ingredients into a blender or food processor and whizz until smooth.

vital statistics

It's the **natural enzymes** in the **pineapple**, particularly bromelain, that help break down and disperse bruises and relieve the pain of **muscle** and joint injuries. The **protein** and **essential fatty acids** from the **almonds**, **vitamin E**, and **B** vitamins from the **wheatgerm**, with **calcium** and **potassium** in the **yoghurt** and **banana**, makes this **healthy nutrition** for everyone and a **power-boost** for athletes of all levels.

Cherry Berry Good

The sweetness of the fruit is contrasted here with the sharp, peppery flavour of rocket. Protective, energizing, cleansing, and restorative, this is the ideal drink for anyone recovering from illness, coping with stress or facing a long, difficult day at work. You may think that rocket doesn't fit well with sweet flavours and be tempted to leave it out; please don't, as it enhances the other aromatic tastes.

Serves 1-2
225g or 8oz fresh cherries
Half a cantaloupe melon
225g or 8oz blueberries
225g or 8oz black, seedless grapes
Half a handful rocket leaves

1 Wash and stone the cherries.
2 Peel and deseed the melon.
3 Wash the blueberries and grapes.
4 Put all the ingredients into a blender or food processor and whizz until smooth.

vital statistics
Rocket contains **tannins** and the **volatile oils** saffronal and cinelle, together with some **pain-relieving** salicylates. **Cherries** are rich in **heart-protective magnesium** and **potassium** and also contain exceptionally large amounts of **cancer-fighting** phytochemicals. Combined with the **antioxidants**, carotenoids, and **vitamin C** in the **grapes** and **blueberries**, this is a recipe for a long and **disease-free** life.

Mango and Lemon Crush

The heady aroma released as you cut into a ripe, juicy mango immediately conjures up images of tropical life, but mango is much more than just taste and smell; it's a rich source of skin-protective and immune-boosting nutrients. Take care, though, if you decide to make this drink for a crowd of friends at a summer barbeque; mango belongs to the same family as poison ivy, and its skin can cause allergic reactions and dermatitis. This isn't a common problem, but it can raise its head if you're handling lots of them in a short space of time. Even if you've never had a skin reaction, do wear gloves when preparing more than two or three.

Serves 1-2
1 large (or 2 medium) ripe mango(es)
1 lemon
About 12 ice-cubes

1 Peel and stone the mango(es).
2 Put through a juicer.
3 Squeeze the juice from the lemon and add to the mango mixture.
4 Crush the ice in a blender and divide between two glasses.
5 Pour on the mango and lemon juice.

vital statistics
Mangoes are a rich source of betacarotene, which the body converts into **vitamin A**, an essential **nutrient** for the skin and **immune system**. Betacarotene is also important in its own right as an antioxidant, as are the other **carotenoids** present in this **fruit**. Heart-protective potassium and **vitamin C** are an additional bonus.

Summer-fruit Punch

Here's another bubbly summer drink that will make any garden party go with a swing. There's certainly enough fruit to make this one healthy as well as enjoyable. Try to get as wide a variety of fruits as you can, including strawberries, raspberries, red- and blackcurrants and blueberries, as these are the richest sources of health-giving nutrients.

Serves 10
200g or 7oz mixed summer fruit
5cm or 2 inches of cucumber
1 lemon
1 bottle rosé wine
1 liqueur glass Cognac
200ml or 7fl oz sparkling
  mineral water
Ice-cubes

1 Wash the fruit, peeling and stoning any if necessary.
2 Slice or cut into bite-size chunks.
3 Peel the cucumber, halve lengthwise, and slice.
4 Put all of the above into a large bowl.
5 Squeeze the juice from the lemon and add to the bowl.
6 Pour in the wine, Cognac, and mineral water.
7 Leave to chill or add ice-cubes before serving.

vital statistics

Again, this is a **party drink** to be enjoyed with friends and family. However, it will be rich in **immune-boosting vitamin C** as well as providing useful amounts of soluble **fibre**. The high concentration of colourful pigments from the **fruit** and the unique **protective** properties of the **pigment** in **red grape skins** (resveratrol) make this a drink which, in moderation, is health-protective.

A Passion for Fruit

This juice drink not only tastes wonderful, it's a real morning eye-opener. It contains enough nutrients to fuel your body's boiler and provide nutritional protection for hours. Vitamins, minerals, and a vast array of plant chemical protectors are things you won't even think about as you enjoy this drink, but they're all there, beavering away to build your defences, nourish your tissues, and protect every cell from potential damage. This should be a regular passion for anyone with arthritis, high blood pressure, poor immunity, skin problems, lethargy or chronic fatigue.

Serves 1-2
6 medium strawberries
2 kiwi fruits
2 passion fruits
2 peaches
1 pomegranate
175g or 6oz seedless grapes

1 Wash and hull the strawberries.
2 Wash the kiwi fruits, but you don't need to peel them.
3 Scoop the flesh from the passion fruits.
4 Wash and stone the peaches – again, they don't need to be peeled.
5 Scrape the flesh and seeds from the pomegranate.
6 Wash the grapes.
7 Put all ingredients through a juicer.
8 Mix thoroughly and serve.

vital statistics

A glass of this **juice** will give you four times your daily requirement of **vitamin C**, as all the fruits are good providers of this **nutrient**. **Betacarotene** and many other carotenoids are here as well to **protect your skin**, vision and overall immune system. **Strawberries**, in particular, contain **anti-arthritic substances**, and the **kiwi fruits** are rich providers of **potassium** and **bioflavonoids**, which protect the heart and blood vessels. The **grapes** not only **provide antioxidants**, but are also a great source of **natural** fruit sugars for instant energy.

Clean

sing

Drinks

Our bodies have the natural ability to cleanse themselves of impurities and waste products, and this process occurs through the kidneys, liver, skin, and respiration. Unfortunately, in today's world we're exposed to atmospheric pollution, unwanted chemicals in our food, and a host of toxic substances in our home environment. To make matters worse, our consumption of healing, cleansing wholefoods such as fresh fruit, vegetables, and wholegrain cereals, has declined alarmingly. The cleansing drinks in this section will help stimulate the body's own vital processes and, at the same time, replenish many of the missing nutrients that are the result of twenty-first-century living.

Two-Flower Treat

People imagine nasty things when it comes to cleansing regimes. Nothing could be further from the truth with this wonderful mixture of elderflowers and nasturtiums. Elderflowers contain cleansing natural chemicals such as tannins and rutin. They're also surprisingly rich in the essential fatty acids that are nature's own anti-inflammatories. The peppery flavour of the nasturtium flowers is the result of the mustard oil, another cleansing and antiseptic natural chemical; its sharpness offsets the sweetness of the elderflower and the rosehip syrup. Combined with the spiciness of ginger, one of the best of all digestive cleansers, and the delicate flavour of the lavender flowers, this makes a fabulous cooling, cleansing drink on a hot summer's day.

Serves 4-5
6 nasturtium flowers
Crushed ice
**2.5cm or 1-inch peeled, grated
  ginger root**
15ml or ½ fl oz pure rosehip syrup
**750ml or 26fl oz organic sparkling
  elderflower pressé**
**5g or ⅛ oz lavender flowers, rubbed
  off the stalk**

1 Put the nasturtium flowers into an ice-cube tray, fill with water, and freeze. If you grow your own, it's worth making up a supply, as they'll keep for at least three months.
2 Fill a large glass tumbler a third full with crushed ice, add the ginger and rosehip and stir well.
3 Pour in the elderflower pressé and float the nasturtium ice-cubes on the top. Sprinkle with the lavender flowers.

Alternative method
If you've got a cocktail shaker, put all the ingredients except the nasturtium cubes in, shake vigorously and pour foaming into the glass, then add the nasturtium cubes and sprinkle with lavender flowers.

vital statistics

This drink is rich in **vitamin C**; one glass provides four times the amount you need for a day. Most of the vitamin C comes from the **rosehip**, but **elderflowers** are a rich source too. **Nasturtiums** are rich in the cleansing **essential oils** myrosin and spilanthol which, as well as their **cleansing** properties, have the benefit of boosting immunity. Most people think of lavender for its essential oils and **perfume** value, but in fact it's delicious added to all sorts of drinks and other foods, and its delicate flavour belies its **potent therapeutic** benefits as a cleansing and protective herb.

Cucumber and Mint Slush

This refreshing, cooling slush is almost tzatziki without the yoghurt. Cucumber isn't rich in nutrients as it's made up mostly of water, but it has long been used as a cleanser – both externally for the skin and internally. It's really the mint that provides the major cleansing benefit, as it is one of the most effective of all digestive aids; because of its detoxing properties, it also helps relieve headaches and migraine. You'll hardly ever see salt added to any of my recipes, but in this instance it does enhance the flavour and helps boost the metabolism.

Serves 1-2
1 large cucumber
4 large stalks mint
Scant tsp natural sea salt
Crushed ice
2 extra mint stalks, for garnish

1 Peel and deseed the cucumber.
2 Put into a blender or food processor with the mint and salt, and whizz until smooth, adding a little water if the consistency is too thick.
3 Chill thoroughly.
4 Serve poured over the crushed ice, with the extra mint stalks for garnish.

vital statistics

Cucumber provides a little **folic acid**, **potassium**, and **silica** but it's here mainly for its gentle diuretic effect, not its nutrients. It's the mint that provides **menthol** and **menthone**, natural **phytochemicals** that are both **antiseptic and cleansing** and also act as a **potent digestive**. Using natural **sea salt** means you get small quantities of **iodine**, which helps improve thyroid function. This, in turn, stimulates the whole **metabolic process** and increases eliminative functions.

Fresh Dill Tea

The subtle flavours of dill combined with the clean, fresh taste of cucumber make a most refreshing cold drink. Dill is both cleansing and mood-enhancing, and it's an excellent remedy for all types of indigestion, especially colic in babies. You can use the leaves sprinkled on any fish dish, added to marinades or sprinkled on cooked vegetables. Steeping a couple of sprigs in a bottle of vinegar makes a useful condiment that is also a digestive aid. Don't waste the rest of the cucumber; use it for traditional cucumber sandwiches to enjoy with your dill tea.

Serves 1-2
6 large stalks dill flowers
Half a cucumber

1 Reserving two of the most attractive dill tops, put the rest into a 600ml (20fl oz) jug of boiling water.
2 Leave for ten minutes.
3 Strain, leave to cool, then chill in the fridge.
4 Meanwhile, strip the peel off the cucumber.
5 Serve the tea with the reserved dill tops and cucumber peel floating on top.

vital statistics

Dill is a source of many **essential oils** and **phytochemicals**, the most important of which are **carvone** and **eugenol**. Surprisingly, it contains **myristicin**, which is also found in **nutmeg** – that is why the dill tea is not only cleansing but also **mood-enhancing** and **stress-relieving**. This tea will also **relieve menstrual pain** and help increase the **flow of milk** in breastfeeding mothers.

Granny's Lemon Barley Water

Lemon barley water has been a traditional cleansing formula of herbalists for hundreds of years. It's particularly effective for all forms of urinary problem, and a great cleansing aid for most skin conditions, particularly those associated with oily skins and recurrent spots. Any of the three herbs enhance the cleansing abilities of this drink, and the high-fibre content of the barley means that one glass can provide up to a third of your daily fibre needs, making this an excellent bowel cleanser as well. Most importantly, it tastes delicious – something most of our grandmothers will have made as a matter of course, but few people today have ever tasted. Try it; I promise it will become one of your family favourites, and the kids will love it.

Serves 4
125g or 4½oz pot barley
55g or 2oz organic demerara sugar
2 organic unwaxed lemons
1,200ml or 40fl oz water
a handful of cowslip flowers,
dandelion leaves or marjoram
Ice-cubes

1 Wash the barley and put it into a large jug.
2 Put the sugar in a bowl. Scrub the lemons with warm water and grate the rind into the sugar; mix together and add to the barley.
3 Bring the water to the boil, pour over the barley, sugar, and lemon rind, stir vigorously and leave to cool.
4 Squeeze the juice from the lemons, add to barley, stir again, and strain through a fine sieve. If you have access to cowslip flowers or dandelion leaves in your own or a friend's garden, they make an unusual addition; if not, you can buy marjoram in the supermarket or grow your own.
5 Serve over lots of ice-cubes for a taste of the 'real thing' – far removed from the over-sweetened, artificial bottled stuff that's commercially available.

vital statistics

The naturally cleansing **plant chemicals** in **cowslips**, **dandelions**, and **marjoram** are what give this drink its real **boost**, though the very high **vitamin C** content is a major **cleansing** factor, too. Because of the **lemon peel**, there is also a rich content of **bioflavonoids**, which are cleansing and protective. As well as the **fibre** from the **barley**, there are modest amounts of **B vitamins**, some **trace minerals**, and a small amount of **protein** as a bonus. As a family drink, this traditional beverage is infinitely **healthier** than any of the canned, bottled or otherwise processed drinks on the market, as it's **free** from all artificial colourings, flavourings, and preservatives.

Fresh Tomato Juice

Once you've tasted this cleansing drink, it's unlikely that you'll ever enjoy the commercial varieties again. Whether in cans or cartons, these nearly always have added salt and lack the 'sweet-and-sour' flavour of the freshly juiced fruits. The acidity of tomatoes is cleansing – even more so when combined with the diuretic properties of celery and the overall detoxing power of garlic. The Worcestershire sauce adds the bite, but if you really want the sting in the tail, why not pour in a measure of vodka?

Serves 1-2
10 ripe tomatoes
4 celery stalks, with leaves
1 small garlic clove
2 dashes Worcestershire sauce

1 Put the tomatoes into a large bowl.
2 Cover with boiling water and leave until cool enough to handle.
3 Slip off the skins.
4 Wash and chop the celery roughly, reserving two sprigs of leaves.
5 Peel the garlic.
6 Put all the ingredients through a juicer.
7 Add the Worcestershire sauce and stir.
8 Chill in the fridge.

vital statistics
Ripe tomatoes are the richest source of the **carotenoid lycopene**, which is highly **protective** against heart disease and prostate cancer. This drink also supplies **betacarotene** and lots of potassium, as well as **vitamins C and E**. You'll get more **potassium** and some **vitamin C** from the **celery**, as well as the **natural diuretics** this vegetable contains.

Fantastic Fennel

The liquorice-like flavour of fennel, combined with the sweetness of apples and pears, imparts a delicious and unusual flavour to this drink. Apples have traditionally been used by natural practitioners as a cleansing and detoxing food, as they have the ability to remove toxic substances from the system. Fennel is a mild diuretic and an extremely good digestive aid; it also has a balancing effect on female hormones.

Serves 1-2
1 carrot
2 large apples
2 pears
1 medium fennel bulb

1 Wash all the ingredients.
2 Peel, top, and tail the carrot if it's not organic.
3 Quarter the apples (but they don't need to be cored).
4 Put everything through a juicer and mix well. Strain if necessary.

vital statistics

Fennel contains the **natural plant chemicals** anethole and fenchone. Although it's traditionally been used for the treatment of **colic** in children, its **diuretic effect** is what makes fennel a useful cleanser. Both **apples** and **pears** are rich in the **soluble fibre**, pectin, which improves digestion and bowel function. Apples are a uniquely **rich source** of ellagic acid, another cleansing **phytochemical**.

Avo Go

This combination of juice and smoothie gets much of its cleansing properties from the pear. Pears are rich in pectin, a soluble fibre that not only improves the body's elimination of cholesterol but also helps stimulate the large bowel and prevent constipation. Ginger has a specific cleansing effect through its stimulation of the peripheral circulation and overall improvement of blood flow. This helps remove waste material so it can be transported to the kidneys and excreted in urine. The live bacteria in the yoghurt improve bowel function and elimination, and the overall cleansing effect of lemon juice rounds everything off.

Serves 1-2

1 large pear
1 garlic clove
1cm or $^1/_2$ inch fresh ginger
50ml or 2fl oz plain live yoghurt
1 medium, ripe avocado
1 lemon

1 Wash the pear and put it through a juicer. Pour the juice into a blender.
2 Peel and chop the garlic.
3 Peel the ginger and grate it finely.
4 Add the garlic and ginger to the blender.
5 Pour in the yoghurt and whizz briefly.
6 Halve and stone the avocado. Scoop out the flesh and add to the blender.
7 Squeeze half the lemon and pour in the juice.
8 Whizz briefly until smooth.

vital statistics

Vitamin E is provided by the **avocado** and is essential for maintaining the healthy **structure** of blood vessels. The **gingerols** and **zingiberene** from the **ginger** are the natural ingredients that **stimulate** the **circulation**. Add to this the cleansing properties of the sulphur compounds in **garlic** and the **high concentration** of **citric acid** in **lemon juice**, and you have a tasty and satisfying **smoothie**.

Lady Windermere's Fan Club

This recipe was given to us by my wife Sally's oldest friend, Diana. She's a keen golfer and a Mancunian and spends a lot of her spare time travelling around the major golf tournaments, helping provide hospitality for the world's top players. According to Diana, this drink is a favourite with lady golfers and all the female golf fans in the north of England. It's the ginger and the lemons that have the cleansing effect – and of course, it tastes even better made with traditional ginger beer.

Serves 2-3
**300ml or 10fl oz chilled
   ginger beer**
300ml or 10fl oz chilled lemonade
2 shots Angostura bitters

1   Just mix everything together and enjoy.

vital statistics
Adding gin might sound appealing, but it probably wouldn't do your golf handicap much good. The **natural** constituents of **ginger** – **gingerols** and **zingiberene** – are **circulatory stimulants** and cleansers while the **vitamin C** and **citric acid** from the **lemons** reinforce the cleansing properties of this drink.

Lime Concentrate

So many commercial cordials are full of artificial chemicals such as colourings, flavourings, and preservatives. To make matters worse, they're often advertised as being sugar-free, but then they contain artificial sweeteners – which certainly are of no benefit to your health. This delicious lime concentrate is very simple to make and you get less than a teaspoon of sugar in a large glass of the drink, so the wonderful tartness of the lime juice is preserved. The gentle cleansing action of the citric acid and vitamin C is just what you need on a hot summer day after a strenuous afternoon in the garden or on the tennis court.

Makes about 1.7 litres or 60fl oz

7 limes
5 lemons
450g or 1lb caster sugar
450ml or 16 floz boiling water
25g or 1oz citric acid

1 Squeeze the juice from the limes and lemons.
2 Mix the juices with all the other ingredients.
3 Stir until the sugar has completely dissolved.
4 Cover in airtight glass containers.
5 Use about two tablespoons to each glass of water.
6 This concentrate keeps in the fridge for several weeks and can be frozen.

vital statistics

Lemons and limes are both rich in **bioflavonoids**, which are important **protectors** of the circulatory system. They also contain **potassium**, **vitamin C**, and the essential oil **limonene**. This combination stimulates the kidneys, increases the flow of urine, and has a gentle **cleansing** action.

Soya with Saffron

Here's a smoothie that's simply bursting with nutritional value. Lots of protein, minerals, plant hormones, and all the digestive protection of honey are present in this mixture. The saffron adds a wonderful colour, but it is also a mood-enhancer and helps improve digestion. Throughout Asia, most women have a daily intake of some form of soya protein, and it is this component of their diets that is believed to protect them against heart disease, osteoporosis, hot flushes, and the other unpleasant symptoms of the menopause in later life.

Serves 1-2
450ml or 16fl oz soya milk
2 heaped tbsp runny honey
1 large pinch saffron
1 tbsp ground almonds
1 tsp slivered almonds

1 Put the first four ingredients into a blender.
2 Whizz until smooth.
3 Serve with the slivered almonds floating on top.

vital statistics

Saffron contains the natural ingredients **saffronal**, **cinelle**, and **crocins** and is known to have anti-depressant and **mood-enhancing properties**. It's main **cleansing** attribute helps to induce **menstruation**, thus preventing the build-up of waste products. The **phytoestrogens** in **soya milk** have a weak hormonal effect that is especially beneficial to women. Although **soya extracts** are now available as tablets, it's far better to get these substances from food than from pills. Like all nuts, **almonds** are a rich source of **vitamin E**, essential fatty acids, and **minerals**.

Popeye's Secret

Popeye's belief that spinach is a great source of muscle-building iron is, unfortunately, not true. There is lots of iron in spinach, but your body can extract hardly any of it due to the oxalic acid that is also present in spinach leaves. However, this wonderful vegetable *is* a very rich source of other nutrients which are especially good for the eyes. Mixed here with diuretic parsley, cleansing melon, and antibacterial sage, it makes a cleansing and healing drink.

Serves 1-2
1 honeydew melon
1 handful baby spinach leaves
4 sage leaves
2 stalks flat-leaf parsley

1 Peel, deseed, and cube the melon.
2 Wash the spinach, sage, and parsley.
3 Put the melon, spinach, and sage leaves into a blender or food processor and whizz until smooth.
4 Tear the leaves off the parsley stalks, chop them finely, and scatter over the juice.

vital statistics

Melon provides **folic acid**, **potassium**, and a little **vitamin A**, **C**, and **B**, but it is renowned in folklore as a **cleansing fruit**. The cancer-fighting **phytochemicals**, large amounts of folic acid, and the **eye-protective carotenoids lutein** and **xeaxanthine** all come from **spinach**, while **sage** provides plant hormones and the powerfully **antiseptic thujone**.

Prune and Apricot Smoothie

Jokingly known as 'nature's little black-coated workers', prunes are an immensely effective cleanser due to their laxative effect. But they are much more than that as, weight for weight, they are the most powerful protective food of all. Regular consumption of prunes really does protect you against premature ageing, heart disease, many forms of cancer, and even wrinkles. Add the nutrients and fibre from apricots and you have a double whammy of a cleanser.

Serves 1-2
6 fresh apricots
250ml or 9fl oz prune juice

1 Wash and stone the apricots.
2 Put into a blender or food processor with the prune juice and whizz until smooth.

vital statistics

Like all dried fruits, **prunes** have a much higher **concentration** of **nutrients** than fresh produce, as all the water has been evaporated. **Prune juice** is rich in betacarotene, **iron**, **B vitamins**, and **potassium**. The fresh **apricots** provide soluble **fibre**, some iron, and lots more **betacarotene**. It's the way these two ingredients stimulate bowel function and **improve digestion** that produces the **cleansing** benefits of this delicious smoothie.

Asparagus Treat

As well as being cleansing, this drink has all the aphrodisiac connotations of asparagus, one of European folklore's great sex foods. Radishes have a specific effect on the liver, improving its efficiency, and the celery is an effective diuretic. The addition of garlic and shallot includes two of the best cleansing and detoxing of all foods. There's even a bonus from the rocket, which is a mild expectorant and adds an extra cleansing boost to the drink.

Serves 1-2

4 spears fresh asparagus
3 carrots
3 radishes, preferably with leaves
2 celery sticks, preferably
with leaves
1 small, fresh uncooked beetroot,
with leaves
1 handful rocket leaves
1 garlic clove
1 small shallot

1 Trim any very woody ends off the asparagus.
2 Peel the carrots, unless they're organic; then they just need topping and tailing.
3 Wash all the vegetables, then peel the garlic and shallot.
4 Put all the ingredients into a juicer.
5 Mix and serve garnished with some of the reserved celery leaves.

vital statistics

This may sounds like a strange mixture, but it has a fresh, **tangy flavour** and provides lots of **betacarotene, volatile oils**, and **tannins** from the **rocket** as well as **folic acid, potassium**, and **asparagine** from the **asparagus**. The radishes provide **natural phytochemicals** that stimulate the gall bladder to produce more bile. Overall, this drink has an abundance of **vitamin C**.

Slim

ming

Drinks

Anyone can lose weight just by keeping his or her mouth shut. If you don't eat, you'll get thin – but you'll also get sick, which is why crash diets don't work. If you restrict your food consumption so much that you lose weight rapidly, you'll soon become deficient in essential nutrients. You'll become tired, irritable, forgetful, and eventually you'll quit in disgust, go on a binge, and put back allthe weight you've lost, plus some. The worst type of diet is onethat excludes whole food groups. The answer is to eat a littleless, exercise a little more, and use foods that help with yourbody's metabolism.

Watermelon and Coconut Chill-out

Here's another juice that provides nutrients you might be missing if you're following a restrictive slimming plan. Coconut milk has unique flavours and aromas and immediately conjures up images of blue skies, even bluer seas, and palm trees. Just the sight of a slice of watermelon is enough to make you think of summer. Add the ginger for a final taste of the tropical Spice Islands.

Serves 2-4
900g or 2lb watermelon
125ml or 4fl oz coconut milk
2 pinches ground ginger

1 Peel, deseed and cube the watermelon.
2 Put into a blender with the coconut milk.
3 Whizz until smooth.
4 Serve with the pinches of ground ginger on top.

vital statistics

Though **watermelon** is not renowned for its **nutrient** content, it's a traditional **cooling food** that does contain **potassium**, **folic acid**, and small amounts of other **vitamins**. **Coconut milk**, however, provides **calcium**, **magnesium**, and **potassium** – all essential **minerals**. The **ginger** is a great **circulatory stimulant**. This juice will **stimulate** your **metabolism** and help speed up the weight-loss process.

Brocolli Breakthrough

Everyone knows how healthy broccoli is, but mixed here with the natural sugars supplied by the apple and pear, and the hot, peppery flavours of watercress, you have a pretty good substitute for lunch and a healthy boost to your weight-loss regime. You'll feel better just looking at the wonderful green colour of this surprisingly enjoyable drink, and I'm sure you'll want to add it to your repertoire of juices – even when you're not trying to lose weight.

Serves 1-2
175g or 6oz broccoli spears
1 apple, preferably Cox's
**   orange pippin, cored**
1 Comice pear, cored
140g or 5oz watercress

1   Wash all the ingredients and put them through a juicer.
2   Chill before serving.

vital statistics
Broccoli is one of the richest sources of **cancer-fighting** phytochemicals. It's also rich in folic acid, **iron**, potassium, riboflavin, and **vitamins A** and C. Watercress is a powerful **antibacterial** food, as it contains **mustard oils** as well as **betacarotene**. It's an absolute must for smokers, as it contains a specific chemical, **phenethyl isothiocyanate**, which protects against lung cancer.

Healthy Sunny Delight

Citrus-fruit juices have always been regarded as an essential part of any slimming plan. Here's a quick, simple shake you can enjoy two or three times a day while following virtually any diet. With no animal fats, the sustaining energy of soya milk, and the instant boost from the fruit sugars in the orange and grapefruit, you'll find this drink a real help. Even for those who aren't great lovers of soya milk, this one tastes really good – why anybody would want to drink a cocktail of chemicals, colourings, artificial sweeteners, and preservatives instead of this healthy offering is quite beyond me.

Serves 1-2
1 grapefruit
1 orange
300ml or 10fl oz soya milk

1 Squeeze the juice from the grapefruit and orange.
2 Mix with the soya milk and serve.

vital statistics

Masses of **vitamin C** and **bioflavonoids** from the **fruit** make this the ideal drink to **boost** your natural resistance and **protect** against **coughs, colds,** and **flu.** This is particularly **important** if you are restricted in your overall food intake, as you may be avoiding other sources of these nutrients. **Soya milk** provides **protein** (as well as **extra calcium** if you choose a fortified variety), together with lots of the **natural** plant hormones that are so important because they protect against **osteoporosis** and many forms of hormone-linked cancers.

Peppery Strawbs

The first time I saw my wife grind black pepper over her strawberries I thought she'd finally flipped. But once I'd tasted this traditional Mediterranean culinary trick, I realized why people did it. The pepper somehow magnifies the flavour of strawberries and makes them even more delicious. Combining that taste with luscious, ripe melon makes this a memorable drink. Because you are using the whole fruit, it's filling and substantial: the perfect alternative as a mid-morning or mid-afternoon sustaining snack.

Serves 1-2
1 cantaloupe melon
225g or 8oz strawberries
Still mineral water
Freshly ground black pepper

1 Peel and deseed the melon.
2 Hull the strawberries.
3 Put them both in a blender and whizz.
4 Thin to the desired consistency with mineral water.
5 Serve with a few twists of pepper in each glass.

vital statistics
Melon is a good source of folic acid, potassium, and **vitamins**. The **strawberries** not only provide generous quantities of **betacarotene**, they're also valuable in the **relief** of arthritic pain; contrary to popular myth which says they're acidic and bad for people with joint problems, they are really **beneficial**. This drink is a good source of **fibre** and quick-release **energy**, thanks to the **natural fruit sugars** that are abundant in these two fruits.

Pepper Me Up

Here's another simple juice that is both unusual and health-giving. Extremely rich in vitamin C, the sweetness of the apples, combined with the hot taste of the watercress, makes this a wonderful digestive aid. Most people feel a bit low from time to time when they're trying to diet; adding the allspice to this drink makes it a real mood-enhancer as well. It's hard to imagine what this tastes like until you've tried it; though it might not sound it, the flavours are terrific.

Serves 1-2

1 orange pepper
1 large bag (140g or 5oz) watercress
3 apples, preferably Cox's
    orange pippins
2 pinches allspice

1   Wash, halve, and deseed the pepper.
2   Wash the watercress and tear off the leaves.
3   Wash, core and quarter the apples.
4   Put all of these ingredients through a juicer.
5   Serve with the allspice sprinkled on top.

vital statistics

Masses of **vitamin C** and betacarotene make this juice another **vital** boost to your natural **immunity**. This is so important, as many people who embark on a **weight-loss** diet find they're more susceptible to every bug that's doing the rounds. As soon as they catch a cold, they have a wonderful excuse to give up the diet. Generous use of this recipe will **protect** you from the **infections** – so you won't have an excuse to quit.

Kiwi with a Kick

What a much-maligned fruit the kiwi fruit is: often dismissed as nothing more than decorative. In fact, not only does it look and taste good, it is also extremely healthy and nourishing, thanks to its high vitamin content. Carrot juice is a traditional part of the naturopathic fasting process, and some people spend huge amounts of money going to a health farm just to drink it by the glassful. You can do it just as well at home – and put the money you save towards a fabulous holiday when you've lost enough weight to look good on the beach.

Serves 1-2
4 kiwi fruits
2 carrots
Half a handful coriander leaves

1 Peel, top and tail the carrots unless they are organic.
2 Wash all the ingredients and put them through a juicer.
3 Mix well and chill before serving.

vital statistics
Weight for weight, a **kiwi fruit** contains **twice** as much **vitamin C** as an **orange**, so one glass of this gives you around four times your daily dose. You'll also get some **vitamin E** and masses of **betacarotene** from the combined benefits of **kiwi fruit** and **carrot**. Adding the **coriander** helps with your body's eliminating processes. It is also extremely **beneficial** to the heart and **circulation** because of its high **coumarin** content.

Rosemaryade

Lemons are one of the traditional ingredients of fasting and detoxing regimes. Their juice is cleansing and mildly diuretic, and this unusual recipe for lemonade produces four large glasses of deliciously cleansing juice. It is infinitely healthier than any slimming drink you could buy and, thanks to the rosemary, it helps boost your mood and improves the memory as a bonus. If you haven't got a rosemary bush in your garden, now's the time to get one, even if it's just in a pot on your doorstep where it will grow very happily all year round.

Serves 1-2

3 lemons
1 tbsp brown sugar
3 sprigs rosemary
400ml or 14fl oz ordinary tap water
850ml or 30fl oz sparkling mineral water

1   Wash the lemons. Grate the rind off and put it into a saucepan with the sugar, rosemary, and tap water.
2   Bring slowly to the boil, simmer for ten minutes, and cool slightly.
3   Add the juice of the lemons.
4   Leave until cold.
5   Strain and add mineral water before serving.

vital statistics

Most of the **vitamin C** from the **lemons** is preserved in this drink, as the juice is added after boiling. It also supplies **bioflavonoids** from the peel as well as the intriguing flavour of **rosemary** mingled with the **tangy** taste of the **lemons**. Drinking plenty of **fluids** is extremely important when you're **slimming**, and here's one way to make sure that you get enough every single day. **Rosemary** contains **volatile oils** and **flavonoids** that have a direct and **beneficial** effect on the **brain**.

Spapple Juice

Almost everyone loves apple juice, and I suppose most of you can imagine combining it with red pepper. But adding *spinach*? I can understand why you may turn up your nose, yet don't knock it until you've tried it. This is a great slimming drink, as it provides a lot of essential nutrients, absolutely no fat, and very few calories. Don't forget the nutmeg – this is what makes you feel at peace with the world when you're struggling to stick to the diet.

Serves 1-2

1 small red pepper
3 apples, preferably Cox's orange pippins
140g or 5oz baby spinach leaves
2 pinches nutmeg

1 Wash the first three ingredients.
2 Deseed the pepper.
3 Quarter and core the apples.
4 Put the first three ingredients through a juicer.
5 Serve with the nutmeg sprinkled on top.

vital statistics

Vitamin C, betacarotene, folic acid, and iron are all here in abundance, thanks to the **red pepper, apples,** and **spinach**. But there's an extra **bonus**, as spinach is a rich source of two **essential carotenoids** which specifically protect the eyes. **Lutein** and **xeaxanthine** are known to help prevent age-related macular degeneration, the most common cause of deteriorating vision in older people. **Nutmeg** contains a wonderful natural chemical called **myristicin**, which is both mood-enhancing and a very mild **hallucinogen**.

Apricot and Passion-fruit Royale

This satisfying and filling drink is a great start to the day as part of any weight-loss regime. There's nothing worse than the terrible mid-morning sugar craving that sends you scuttling for the biscuit tin when you're desperately trying to lose a few pounds. Add this drink to your breakfast and you'll get a great mixture of instant and slow-release energy that will carry you through to your healthy lunch break.

Serves 2-3
2 passion fruits
8 apricots
400ml or 14fl oz soya milk

1 Scoop the pulp from the passion fruits and press through a sieve to remove the pips. Reserve some of the pips.
2 Peel and stone the apricots.
3 Put the fruit into a blender with the soya milk.
4 Whizz until smooth.
5 Serve with the reserved pips floating on top.

vital statistics

The danger of any restricted weight-loss plan is that you can easily miss out on **nutrients** as well as calories. Here you'll get plenty of **vitamin C** from the fresh **apricots** and **passion fruits**, together with their rich supply of protective **betacarotene** and other **carotenoids**. You'll get **minerals**, too, and from the **soya milk** you get the **natural** plant hormones that are particularly useful for all women **slimmers**. These help to balance and regulate your own hormone **metabolism** and control the **ups** and **downs** of weight associated with both the menstrual cycle and the menopause.

What a Plum!

This is tomato juice with a difference. It mixes the traditional Mediterranean flavours of tomato and basil with the sharpness of lemon juice, the sweetness of carrot, and the distinctive taste of celery. It is a real morning eye-opener and makes an interesting alternative to the usual breakfast fruit juices. It's not only refreshing and cleansing, but an enormously rich source of a wide range of nutrients.

Serves 1-2
1 carrot
4 large, ripe plum tomatoes
1 stick celery, with leaves
1 handful basil
Juice of 1 lemon
Freshly ground black pepper

1 Wash the first four ingredients.
2 Top, tail and peel the carrot if it's not organic.
3 Put all the ingredients straight into a juicer.
4 Mix well and add the lemon juice.
5 Serve with a twist of pepper.

vital statistics

Apart from the obvious **betacarotene** in the **tomatoes** and **carrot**, you'll get masses of **potassium**, lots of **vitamins C** and **E, folic acid**, and **magnesium** from this drink. Four ripe **tomatoes** also provide a massive boost of **lycopene**, which is one of the most powerful protectors against **prostate cancer** and **heart disease. Celery** is a mild **diuretic** and will help get rid of excessive fluid, while **basil** is one of the best of all the calming, **mood-enhancing** culinary herbs.

Resto

rative Drinks

Most of us succumb to the occasional illness. Usually these problems are comparatively minor and short-lived, but sometimes they may be catastrophic in their consequences. Surprisingly, some people take months to recover their full vigour after a simple cold, while others can be back on top within weeks of major surgery. Once again, the answer can be found in the Pandora's box of nutrition. Lift the lid and if you find instant meals, convenience foods, takeaways, refined carbohydrates, and loads of artificial additives, then you'll know that the person this box belongs to will suffer the most. If you discover piles of fruit and vegetables, wholegrain cereals, plenty of fish and other good proteins, lots of pulses, and a generous serving of soya-based foods, you'll find the person who will recover the fastest.

Espresso Sublime

Ice-cream is easy to eat and, as long as it's proper dairy ice-cream without all the chemicals and added synthetic fats, it's also excellent food for invalids. The coffee flavour and small amount of Drambuie in this drink turns a child's treat into a sophisticated, adult-friendly, medicinal food. Use organic dark-chocolate powder and a little pure vanilla essence for the children.

Serves 1-2
300ml or 10fl oz cold, strong, dark coffee, preferably espresso
75ml or around 3fl oz full-fat milk
3 tbsp Drambuie
2 scoops good-quality vanilla ice-cream, preferably organic

1 Mix together the coffee, milk, and Drambuie.
2 Pour into glasses and top with the scoops of ice-cream.

vital statistics

Yes, this one does contain **caffeine**, but as long as you're not one of the small number of people who are extremely **sensitive** to this chemical, it can provide a good **energy boost** if you're feeling low after an illness. **Organic** dairy **ice-cream** is an excellent source of calories, **calcium**, **vitamins A** and **D**, and small amounts of **B vitamins** – all of which help restore you to good health as quickly as possible, in an extremely enjoyable way.

Almond and Raspberry Milk

This is a wonderful sick-room remedy. Fifty years ago, every cookbook had chapters on food for convalescents – but not anymore. Like all nuts and seeds, almonds are a considerable source of body-building nutrients. Milk is easily digestible and, to most people, palatable, so it's a simple way of rebuilding rundown bodies. Add all the protective antioxidants and the high ORAC score of raspberries for a powerhouse restorative beverage.

Serves 1-2
25g or 1oz ground almonds
400ml or 14fl oz semi-skimmed milk
10 raspberries

1 Wash the ground almonds in a sieve.
2 Drain thoroughly.
3 Put into a jug and mix thoroughly with the milk.
4 Serve with the raspberries on top.

vital statistics

All **nuts** and **seeds** contain every **nutrient** needed to produce the next generation of plants. **Almonds** are no exception, providing well-absorbed quantities of **protein, B vitamins, zinc,** and **healing essential fatty acids.** The **milk** contains easily used calories for restorative energy, while the **raspberries** are rich in **vitamin C** and protective **phytochemicals.**

Blueberry Fool

Whoever heard of cheesecake in a health book? Yet this is basically cheesecake without the cake. The wonderful protection that every cell in your body gets from blueberries, the rebuilding calcium and protein from the milk, vitamins A and D, some of the Bs, and even more calcium from the ricotta turn this extremely pleasant and simple recipe into a potent healing potion.

Serves 1-2
280g or 10oz blueberries
115g or 4oz ricotta cheese
About 125ml or 4fl oz semi-skimmed milk

1 Wash the blueberries and put them and the ricotta into a blender or food processor.
2 Whizz until smooth.
3 Thin with the milk to the desired consistency.

vital statistics
Having an extremely high ORAC **antioxidant** score, **blueberries** are one of the most **protective** and **restorative** of all foods. With lots of **calcium** needed to rebuild the bones of anyone who's had a few weeks in bed and the **well-absorbed nutrients** and low fat content of the semi-skimmed **milk**, this is a **healthy** and ideal treat for men, women, and children of all ages.

Who are you Calling a Prune?

You can enjoy the complex flavours of this recipe as a thickish juice or as a really thick smoothie, depending on your taste. But however you like it, the prunes, apples, and grapes will greatly enhance your body's restorative powers. Adding the cheese makes it quite substantial and a valuable source of body-building nutrients for anyone under the weather.

Serves 1-2
10 pitted, ready-to-eat prunes
1 large dessert apple
250g or 9oz white seedless grapes
125ml or 4fl oz mascarpone cheese
Still mineral water

1 Put the prunes in a bowl, just cover with freshly boiled water, and leave to soak for 30 minutes.
2 Meanwhile, wash the apple and grapes, core and quarter the apple and put it through a juicer with the grapes, saving a few of the grapes for decoration.
3 Put the juice into a blender.
4 Drain the prunes and add them to the juice.
5 Whizz until smooth.
6 Add the mascarpone and whizz again.
7 If the mixture seems too thick for your taste, add mineral water until you get the required consistency.
8 Serve with the grapes floating on top.

vital statistics

Prunes have the **highest ORAC** score of any food. The **prunes** alone in this recipe will give you well over the 5,000 of these **protective antioxidant** units that are the optimum quantity for a day. The natural **sugars** from the **grapes** and the **cholesterol-lowering pectins** in the **apple juice** just add to the beneficial nutritional properties that you'll get in every glass. Include the **calcium, zinc,** and **protein** from the **mascarpone** and you've got a drink fit for Lazarus.

Pineapple and Coriander Cup

This is another delicious, refreshing, and restorative summer drink, but it's also great as a digestive aid after any large meal, such as those we tend to have on Christmas Day, Boxing Day or Thanksgiving. As long as your pineapple is ripe, the flavour will be deliciously sweet but offset by the sharp taste of the coriander. Both coriander and pineapple are renowned repairers, and pineapple has the added benefit of healing bruises and improving digestion. This is also a great drink for anyone with a sore throat.

Serves 1-2

1 small pineapple
2 stalks coriander
75g or around 3oz brown caster sugar
500ml or 18fl oz apple juice
Water to dilute, if necessary

1 Peel the pineapple and cut out the woody core.
2 Chop the pineapple very finely.
3 Tear the leaves off the coriander and chop them very finely.
4 Put the pineapple and coriander into a jug and stir in the sugar.
5 Leave to rest in the fridge for at least two hours.
6 Pour on the apple juice and dilute with water to achieve the required consistency.

vital statistics

Pulling the spiky leaves out of the top of a **pineapple** to test its **ripeness** is one of the few old wives' tales that isn't true. Pineapples stop ripening the minute you cut them from the tree; leaving them to **soften** in your **fruit basket** means just waiting for them to rot. The ripest pineapples have a high content of **juice** and **sugar** and feel really **heavy** for their size. Always pick them up before buying and if they don't feel heavy, leave them alone. **Pineapples** are an exceptional source of the enzyme **bromelain**, which is extremely **healing** and **repairing**. Mixed with the **phytochemicals** in **coriander** and the soluble **fibre** in cloudy **apple juice,** this makes a potent drink indeed.

Yummy Kiwi

Kiwi fruit is a great source of vitamin C and other nutrients. Although real dairy ice-cream contains some fat, it's also good for your bones and very cooling. Whizzed together, this mixture turns a delicate shade of green, has the consistency of single cream, and offers the most delicious taste. It's another treat suitable for adults and children, and is perfect taken to a picnic in a thermos.

Serves 1-2
2 fresh kiwi fruits, peeled and quartered
125ml or 4fl oz semi-skimmed milk
1 large scoop vanilla ice-cream, preferably organic

1   Peel and quarter the kiwi fruits.
2   Put all the ingredients into a blender or food processor and whizz until smooth.

vital statistics

Weight for weight, a **kiwi fruit** contains twice as much **vitamin C** as an orange and is also a good source of **betacarotene** and other **carotenoids**. It is exceptionally high in **potassium**, which is important for a healthy **heart**, and contains no fat and virtually no salt – so it's even more beneficial to the heart and **circulation**. Using **semi-skimmed milk** reduces the overall fat content, in spite of the ice-cream.

Lemon and Ginger Tea

I'm not a great lover of the quick fix – especially as this usually means covering up the symptoms and sweeping the problem under the carpet. But when you're feeling a bit low, run down, and one degree under, here's a quick fix that I really do recommend. Nothing works quite as well as this extremely simple but deliciously stimulating drink. The cleansing citrus flavour of the lemon is an ideal combination with the tropical heat of ginger. Together they provide an almost instant mood boost: raising energy and gingering up the circulation.

Serves 2-3
2.5cm or 1-inch fresh ginger root
600ml or 20fl oz boiling water
1 lemon

1 Peel and grate the ginger root.
2 Cover with the boiling water.
3 Add the juice of half the lemon and leave to cool.
4 Put in the fridge to chill.
5 Strain and serve with slices taken from the other lemon half.

vital statistics

Lemons provide much more than just **vitamin C**, as they're also a rich source of **natural bioflavonoids** which help **strengthen** and **protect** the walls of your **blood vessels**. Add **ginger's** essential natural oils (**gingerols** and **zingiberine**), and you'll **benefit** from centuries of ancient wisdom. Ginger has been used in Chinese medicine for several thousand years and is one of the most **effective stimulants** in the ancient herbal repertoire. Unlike caffeine or alcohol, this drink has **no side effects** and doesn't leave you feeling even more deflated within the hour.

Mascarpone and Mint

Mint and mascarpone is a surprising combination of tastes. If you're in need of restoration, however, this will certainly do the trick as it will provide you with strength, energy, and nutrients along with the added bonus of the mint to help digestion.

Serves 2
2 large sprigs of mint
250ml or 9fl oz mascarpone cheese
150ml or 5fl oz semi-skimmed milk

1 Strip the leaves off the mint, leaving two top sprigs whole.
2 Put the rest of the ingredients into a blender and whizz until smooth.
3 Serve with the reserved mint sprigs on top.

vital statistics

Mint's essential **oils**, such as **menthone** and **menthol**, are protective, mood-enhancing, and great aids to the **digestion**. **Mint** improves the breakdown and absorption of **nutrients**, as well as preventing and relieving indigestion, wind, and general abdominal discomfort. The **muscle-** and **bone-building** benefits of **milk** and **cheese** are exceptional, and make this a restorative must for anyone with broken bones, hiatus hernia, reflux problems or hyperacidity.

One for the Day After the Night Before

Self-inflicted illnesses such as hangovers don't deserve much sympathy, but having seen so much suffering over the years, I include this recipe as a gesture of sympathy for those overcome by weakness the night before. No doubt most of you were led into temptation by others, so here's the perfect way to restore yourself to some semblance of functioning humanity.

Serves 1-2
2 camomile tea bags
Ice-cubes
125ml or 4fl oz apple juice
1 lemon
½ tsp slippery elm bark
1 banana

1 Make two mugs of tea with the tea bags and add ice-cubes to cool.
2 Add the apple juice.
3 Squeeze the juice from the lemon and add to the mugs.
4 Stir in the slippery elm bark.
5 Peel and finely slice the banana and float on the juice.

vital statistics

Slippery **elm bark** is a traditional herbalist's **remedy** for **upset stomachs** of all kinds, and there's not much worse than one upset by a **surfeit** of alcohol. The **healing** chemicals in **apples** are renowned for their **soothing effect** on the stomach, and **camomile** tea really helps with the **headache**, **nausea**, and general wretchedness of the hangover. Adding the easily digested **banana** provides a little solid **nourishment** that your delicate system will be able to handle with ease.

Pep Yourself Up

All of the red, yellow, and orange vegetables contain the chemicals your body needs for the replacement of damaged cells. In any illness or at times of excessive stress, overwork, and difficult life situations, your body suffers. This really savoury and delicious juice could make all the difference.

Serves 1-2

1 small red pepper
3 carrots
1 small, fresh uncooked beetroot, preferably with leaves
1 handful flat-leaf parsley, with stems
1 handful watercress leaves

1 Wash and deseed the pepper.
2 Wash the carrots; they don't need peeling, topping or tailing unless they're non-organic.
3 Put all of the vegetables and herbs through a juicer, reserving a few watercress leaves.
4 Mix thoroughly and serve with a few watercress leaves on top.

vital statistics

Parsley is a **natural diuretic** that helps the body eliminate waste products. The red colouring in **beetroot** is produced by a natural ingredient that improves the **oxygen-carrying** capacity of the blood, while the **peppers** and **carrots** are a huge source of **restorative carotenoids** and **vitamin C. Watercress** is one of nature's most powerful **cancer-fighters**, with a very specific effect on lung tissue.

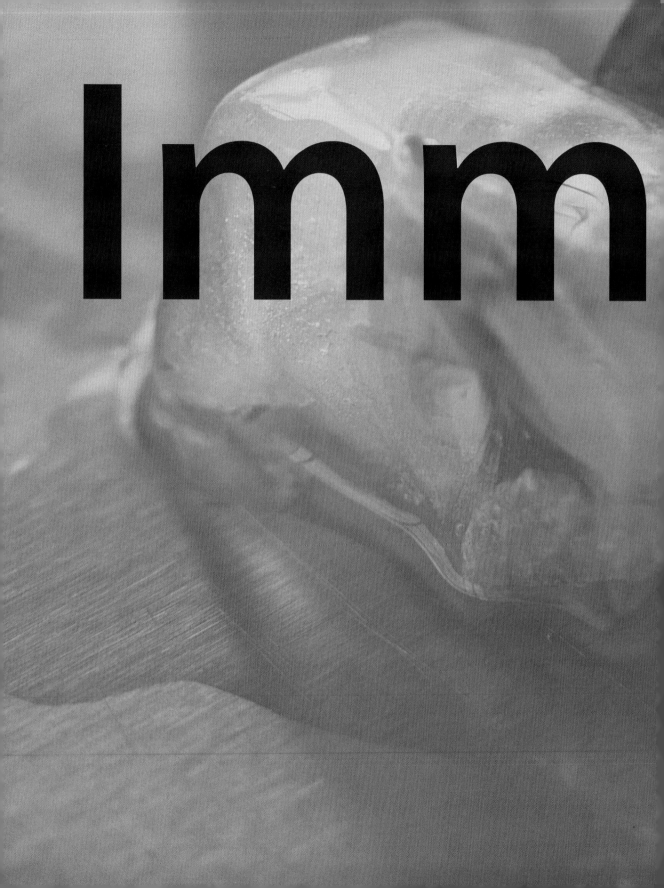

Imm

unity
Drinks

Have you ever wondered why it is that whenever an epidemic of flu sweeps through your community, there's always a handful of people who don't succumb? It's because these are the men, women, and children whose immune systems are working at peak performance to protect their bodies against invading bacteria and viruses. The way to boost your own immunity is to make sure you get all the nutrients that are essential for this amazing protective mechanism to function at its maximum ability. Of course, you need all the vital vitamins and minerals, but your body must also have the protective good bacteria, powerful and immune-boosting phytochemicals, and the right balance of essential fats, proteins, and carbohydrates. Here they are, in some simple and delicious cooling drinks.

Help, I'm a Chocoholic!

We all feel happier after eating chocolate, and just being happy gives your immune system a jump-start. But there's more to it than that; chocolate is a source of immune-boosting phytochemicals. Bananas are nature's miracle fast-food, providing energy and essential nutrients that the body needs in order to stay fit and well. The benefits of friendly bacteria, a good dose of your daily requirement of calcium, and the mood-enhancing benefits in nutmeg mean you'll soon be back for more of this one.

Serves 2
1 banana
400ml or 14fl oz plain live yoghurt
**1 heaped tbsp organic chocolate
  powder**
2 small pinches of nutmeg

1 Peel and chop the banana.
2 Put the banana into a blender with the yoghurt and chocolate powder.
3 Whizz until smooth.
4 Serve with the nutmeg sprinkled on top.

Note
This delicious smoothie works just as well if you substitute six large strawberries for the banana.

vital statistics
Theobromine from **chocolate** and **myristicine** from **nutmeg** are two plant chemicals that have **mood-enhancing** properties. **Nutmeg** also **helps sleep** and **improves digestion**, both of which are good for the **immune system**. Beneficial bacteria in live **yoghurt** produce by-products that are absorbed directly through the intestinal lining and play a very important part in strengthening **natural immunity**. **Potassium** from the **banana** and **calcium** from the yoghurt are just an added bonus.

Green Tea with Apples

If you're not a regular user of green tea, you'll find this flavour a lot weaker than your usual Indian tea blend. The subtle taste goes well with the sweetness of the apple juice and the tartness of lemons. Green tea, so popular in the Far East, has been used medicinally as an immunity-building drink for thousands of years. Now's your chance to experience both the flavour and the benefits of this delicious Oriental brew.

Serves 2

2 green-tea tea bags
1 small eating apple,
   preferably Cox's orange pippin
Half a lemon
75ml or around 3fl oz apple juice

1 Put the tea bags into two large heatproof glasses.
2 Half-fill with boiling water and leave to brew for ten minutes. Remove the tea bags.
3 Leave to cool completely.
4 Core the apple and cut into thin slices.
5 Squeeze the juice from the lemon.
6 Add the lemon and apple juices to the tea.
7 Serve with the apple slices on top.

vital statistics

Although it's now known that all types of **tea** contain **immune-boosting** antioxidants, scientists have been studying the **health-giving** properties of **green tea** for a number of years. **Apples** supply the cholesterol-lowering properties of pectin, a special type of **soluble fibre**; they also contain **malic acid** for **digestion** and **potassium** to keep **blood pressure down**. Add the **vitamin C** present in the **juices**, and you have a great health-giving beverage.

Boozy Raspberries

It's hard to believe that anything tasting this good can be so healthy. But trust me: it's true. Summer or winter, this smoothie will give your immune system a massive boost, and it's just as nice and effective made with frozen fruit. If you are using frozen raspberries, let them thaw a bit so they're just softening before you whizz them. Vitamin C and other protective nutrients in the raspberries are complemented by the beneficial bacteria in the live yoghurt. The vibrant colour from the blackcurrant liqueur makes it look as good as it tastes.

Serves 2
75g or about 3oz raspberries
350ml or 12fl oz plain live yoghurt
2 tbsp blackcurrant liqueur

1 Put all the ingredients into a blender or food processor and whizz until smooth.
2 Serve chilled.

vital statistics
Raspberries are a fairly good source of immune-boosting **vitamin C** and also have a very high **ORAC** score. Just 100g provide 1,220 ORACs – almost as much as the average UK resident gets from his or her **total food** intake in a day. It's this amazing **antioxidant** factor, together with the immune-boosting **probiotic** bacteria from the **yoghurt**, that supplies the huge **immunity** charge in every portion.

Mangobano Smoothie

Make this a family favourite for breakfast and you'll send them all off to school, college or work with a shot in the arm for their natural resistance. This is really valuable during the autumn and winter months, when we are all exposed to other people's flu- and cold-causing organisms. It makes a great sustaining smoothie when it's going to be a long time before the next meal, and a perfect pre-exercise recipe when you couldn't eat a meal but do need some extra energy and stamina.

Serves 2
1 large mango
2 bananas
400ml or 14fl oz plain live yoghurt

1 Peel, stone, and cube the mango.
2 Peel and slice the bananas.
3 Put all the ingredients into a blender and whizz until smooth.

vital statistics
You'll get lots of resistance-building **betacarotene**, **flavonoids**, **potassium**, antioxidants, and **vitamin C** from the **mango**; plenty of potassium, fast- and slow-release energy, and **vitamin B_6** from the **bananas**; and more resistance-building bacteria from the **yoghurt**. Peeling the **mango** is well worth the effort.

Veggie Wake-up Call

Mixing sweet pawpaws with vegetable juice may sound a bit strange, but there's nothing odd about the finished smoothie. Here you've got all the benefits to your immune system from some of the healthiest of fruits, the nutrients in the mixed vegetable juice, the spiciness of ginger and the creamy smoothness of a good, live, natural yoghurt – all this and improved resistance, too.

Serves 2
2 pawpaws
150ml or 5fl oz vegetable juice
150ml or 5fl oz apple juice
1 tsp ground ginger
50ml or 2fl oz plain live yoghurt

1 Peel and deseed the pawpaws.
2 Put all the ingredients into a blender or food processor and whizz until smooth.

vital statistics

As well as the **carotenoids** you'd expect from **fruit** the colour of **pawpaws**, there's a special benefit to be gained from the digestive enzyme **papain**, which they also contain. This improves the efficiency of **digestion** and helps ensure that the **maximum nutritional benefit** is extracted from the food you eat. The **ground ginger** is a surprising **immune-booster** as the **gingerols** in this extraordinary root will help "ginger up" your entire system.

Spuds 'R' Us

You may never have thought of juicing a sweet potato, but this really is one of the most immunity-building and cancer-preventative foods around. Mixing sweet potatoes with the flavours of kiwi fruit and orange juice makes a delicious combination that tastes better than it sounds and is a powerful protector against short-term infections and long-term disease.

Serves 2
1 large sweet potato
3 kiwi fruit
300ml or 10fl oz freshly squeezed orange juice

1 Wash the sweet potato and peel the kiwi fruits.
2 Put the potato and kiwi fruit through a juicer.
3 Add the orange juice and mix well.

vital statistics

Huge amounts of **vitamin C** from the **kiwi fruits** and **orange juice** are coupled with **betacarotene** and a range of other **essential carotenoids**, as well as the cancer-fighting **phytochemicals** in the **sweet potato**. The **orange juice** also provides another group of chemicals called **bioflavonoids**, which play an important role in the **protection** of your blood vessels. This mixture is an all-round protector that increases your **natural resistance** to bugs and degenerative diseases.

Spiced Coconut

Coconut milk is easily available even in your local supermarket, so there's no excuse for not trying this exotic, spicy way to protect yourself from all sorts of infections. The heady scents of coconut and cloves are redolent of tropical islands, blue seas, and sunshine, and thinking of that is enough to make you feel better on its own. This takes just seconds to prepare, but do take the time to savour the taste and soak up the benefits.

Serves 2-3

300ml or 10fl oz coconut milk
150ml or 5fl oz full-fat milk
1 tbsp runny honey
2 tsp ground cloves, plus a little
  to serve

1 Put the coconut milk, ordinary milk, honey, and cloves in a blender and whizz well.
2 Serve with an extra pinch of ground cloves on each glass.

vital statistics

Plenty of **calcium**, **magnesium**, **potassium**, **protein**, and modest amounts of **vitamins B** and **D** come from the **coconut** and **whole milk**. The **cloves** provide aromatic **essential oils** that are both **healing** and **antibacterial**. Even the **honey** has protective benefits, as it contains traces of **natural antibiotics** produced by the bees – which is why honey never goes mouldy.

Tango Smoothie

This tastes and smells wonderful, and even when fresh peaches are not available, it's pretty good made with canned ones as long as they're in pure juice or water and not sugar syrup. The unique taste of lime contrasts well with the sweeter, heavier flavours of the other fruits, and when the yoghurt is added it takes on a wonderful creamy consistency. For a thicker smoothie, try using traditional Greek yoghurt or adding some mascarpone or crème fraîche.

Serves 2
2 large peaches
2 large mangoes
1 lime
450ml or 16fl oz plain live yoghurt

1 Stone the peaches.
2 Peel and stone the mangoes.
3 Put both fruits through a juicer.
4 Cut two or three slices from the lime, then squeeze the juice from the rest.
5 Mix the lime, peach, and mango juices with the yoghurt.
6 Serve with the reserved lime slices on top.

vital statistics

The **peaches** and **mangoes** provide a large injection of **betacarotene** and lots of other **carotenoids**, which specifically **protect** the skin and mucous membranes and help **boost immunity**, while an extra **vitamin C** boost comes from the **lime**. The **yoghurt** provides **resistance-boosting** friendly bacteria that live in the intestine, where they both help **destroy** unwanted **bugs** and have a direct effect on the general **immune system**.

24-Hour Detox Fast

Here is a simple plan for a 24-hour detox fast. But first, a word of warning; this is not suitable for diabetics, and if you have some other serious illness or are currently taking prescribed medication, do check with your doctor before trying it (although it should be suitable for almost everyone). Use this for an occasional short, sharp cleansing process or – better still – do it once a month to keep your body's toxic load to a minimum.

It's best to start this fast on a day when you're not working, and it's much more effective if on the day before, you keep off alcohol, coffee, red meat, and all dairy products. The day after the detox do the same, then return to your normal but (hopefully healthier) eating patterns.

Drink at least six glasses of water, and as much herb or weak China tea as you like throughout the day. Don't add milk, sugar or sweeteners and avoid fizzy water, canned drinks, squashes, alcohol, and coffee.

First thing in the morning, make up a jug of parsley tea. Pour 850ml or 30fl oz of boiling water over a generous handful of chopped parsley. Cover, leave for ten minutes, strain, refrigerate, and drink throughout the day. Parsley tea is a mild diuretic which eliminates excess fluid and helps the cleansing process. Make sure it's all gone by bedtime.

On waking
A large glass of hot water with a thick slice of organic, unwaxed lemon.

Breakfast
A large glass of hot water with a thick slice of organic unwaxed lemon.
A glass of Pawpaw and Ginger Refresher (*see* page 17).
A cup of camomile tea.

Mid-morning
Another large glass of hot water with a thick slice of organic, unwaxed lemon.

Lunch
A large glass of What a Plum! (*see* page 91).
Mint tea.

Mid-afternoon
A large glass of hot water with a thick slice of organic, unwaxed lemon.

Supper
A Passion for Fruit (*see* page 55).
Camomile tea.

Evening
Pep Yourself Up (*see* page 106).

Bedtime
Lime-blossom tea.

Nature's Medicine Cabinet

Condition	Healing foods	Effect
Acne	Carrots	Are rich in betacarotene, essential for healthy skin
	Tomatoes	Are the best source of lycopene, a skin-friendly nutrient
	Garlic, onions	Are antibacterial
Anaemia	All citrus fruits	Contain vitamin C, which improves absorption of iron
	Watercress, figs	Contain iron
Anxiety	Basil, rosemary, camomile	Contain calming essential oils
	Dairy products	Encourage the brain's production of feel-good hormones
Arthritis	Celery, strawberries	Improve elimination of uric acid
Asthma	Garlic, onions (shallots)	Are natural decongestants
	Watercress	Is rich in unique lung-protective chemicals
Bronchitis	Garlic, onions	Are powerful antibacterials and decongestants
	Coriander, thyme	Are expectorant and decongestant
Bruising	Pineapple	Contains bromelain, an enzyme that breaks down blood clots
Chilblains	Basil, garlic, ginger coriander	Have specific natural chemicals that improve circulation
Cholesterol	Garlic, peanuts, peanut butter	Help the body to eliminate cholesterol
	Citrus fruits	Contain bioflavonoids, which strengthen and protect blood vessels
Chronic fatigue	Basil, sage, nutmeg	Are mood-enhancing
	Banana, apricot	For potassium, vitamin B_6, and energy
	Peanuts, peanut butter	For slow-release energy
Cystitis	Garlic	Is antibacterial and antifungal
	Celery, parsley	Are gentle, cleansing diuretics
	Cranberry juice	Protects the bladder from bacteria that cause cystitis
	Lemon barley water	Is a traditional folk remedy for this condition
Flatulence	Fennel, mint, coriander	All these herbs contain essential volatile oils which improve digestion and reduce flatulence
Fluid retention	Parsley	Is one of the most effective natural diuretics; use generously
	Celery	Is a gentle diuretic
Heartburn	Mint, dill, fennel	Contain natural antacid essential oils
	Live yoghurt	Provides probiotic bacteria, which aid digestion
	Carrots	Are traditional naturopathic foods for all digestive upsets

Condition	Healing Foods	Effect
Heart disease	Blueberries, passion fruit pomegranate, beetroot black grapes	Are extremely rich in protective antioxidants
	Avocadoes	Contain artery-protective vitamin E
Hypertension	Garlic	Phytochemicals in garlic are beneficial to good blood pressure
	Parsley, celery	Reduce fluid retention
	Avocadoes	Contain artery-protective vitamin E
Influenza	Ginger	Speeds the elimination of toxins
	Honey	Soothes a sore throat and cough
	Lemons and limes	Are extremely rich in Vitamin C
Insomnia	Lettuce	Contains natural sleep-inducing chemicals
	Basil	Has calming essential oils
	Milk, yoghurt, fromage frais	Supply sleep-inducing tryptophans
Laryngitis	Sage, rosemary	Contain essential oils that are specifically antibacterial to the bugs that commonly cause throat problems
Menstrual problems	Sage	Helps regulate hormone levels
	Celery, parsley	Are diuretic and help with fluid retention
	Cherries, bananas	Are rich in potassium
	Soya milk	Contains plant oestrogens
Mouth ulcers	Garlic	Helps with healing
	Yoghurt	Its good bacteria helps prevent ulcers
	Basil, rosemary	Are stress-relievers: important as ulcers are mostly stress-induced
Raynaud's syndrone	Basil, ginger, garlic coriander	Help improve circulation
Restless legs	Watercress, figs	Contain iron to prevent anaemia, a common cause of the condition
	Bananas	For potassium to prevent cramp
	Mango, pawpaw	For enzymes and betacarotene for healthy blood vessels
SAD	Basil, rosemary	Contain mood-enhancing essential oils
	Nutmeg	Contains myristicin to make you feel good
	Milk, yoghurt, bananas	Increase levels of mood-enhancing tryptophan
Sinusitis	Onions, garlic	The alliums are powerful antibacterials and decongestants
	Coriander, ginger, cloves	Are expectorant and decongestant
Varicose veins	Ginger	Stimulates and improves circulation
	Avocadoes	Provide vein-protecting vitamin E
	Dark cherries, blueberries passion fruit, pomegranate	Contain protective antioxidants and bioflavonoids

Index